THE RESEARCH ESSAY

a guide to essays and papers

Hugh Robertson

The Research Essay
A Guide to Essays and Papers

Fifth Edition

Copyright© 1985, 1991, 1995, 1999, 2001.
Piperhill Publications, Ottawa. All rights reserved.

www.piperhill.ca

ISBN 0-9693068-7-3

Printed and bound in Canada.

Canadian Cataloguing in Publication Data

Robertson, Hugh, 1939–
The research essay: a guide to essays and papers

5th ed.
First 2 editions published under title: The research essay: a guide to papers, essays, projects.
Includes bibliographical references and index.
ISBN 0-9693068-7-3

1. Report writing. 2. Research. I. Title.

LB2369.R633 2001   808'.066   C2001-900089-8

Cover and Interior Design: Avante Graphics & Sharper Images
Copy Editor: Margo Whittaker

This book was manufactured in Canada using acid-free and recycled paper.

CONTENTS

ACKNOWLEDGEMENTS

The Research Essay was first published in 1985. Since then it has undergone numerous changes and improvements. These improvements are largely due to a number of people who have offered practical suggestions and perceptive comments. I would like to pay tribute to the following persons for their counsel and contributions: Ian Andrews, Dr. Jeanne Beck, Professor Aleksandra Bennett, Professor Sharon Cook, Professor William Dray, John Einarson, Professor Alan Gillmor, Ludi Habs, Jeanette Jarosz, Mike Jones, Matt Labarge, Frances Montgomery, Alyssa Novick, Hugh Penton, Professor Rod Phillips, Professor George Roseme, Suzanne St-Jacques, and Jake Selwood.

Betsey Baldwin, Tony Horava, Sacha Richard, and Mark Thompson have been generous in sharing their experience and expertise in preparing the fifth edition. My grateful thanks to them.

Dedicated to the memory of
Wayne Alexander Howell, M.D.

〜

INTRODUCTION

Essay writing is a central part of humanities and social sciences courses from secondary school to graduate school. Writing essays is not always an easy task. However, there are procedures to make it less difficult and to transform the process into a stimulating learning experience. *The Research Essay* takes you step by step through the entire process of writing an academic essay or term paper — from conception to completion. Using a single example, this manual will guide you through launching the essay, locating sources, gathering ideas and information, organizing the material, and composing a thesis or argument.

One of the initial problems facing students is the array of terms associated with writing assignments. These terms range from extended essays and research projects to themes and term papers. An essay is not a creative writing assignment nor an exposition of factual information. It is neither a narrative chronicle, a biographical report, nor a descriptive composition. **An essay has an argument, or point of view, or thesis.** It is your point of view imprinted on an essay or term paper that distinguishes it from other types of writing — no argument, no essay.[1]

The process described in this manual is the result of many years of teaching students of various ages. It is a practical process that has been thoroughly tried and tested. It is not a rigid formula, but a flexible model that you can adapt to suit your own individual needs, whether you prefer to use the latest computer technology or a more traditional approach. While a history topic is used to demonstrate the process, the method can be used for essays and term papers in most humanities and social sciences subjects. Although the manual focuses on the essay and emphasizes the importance of having an argument or thesis, the method can also be modified for descriptive and narrative assignments, reports, book reviews, examinations, and oral presentations, such as seminars.

The academic essay is the basis of much professional writing: legal briefs, business reports, judicial decisions, arts reviews, newspaper editorials, and scholarly articles are all variations on the theme of the academic essay. Essay writing develops many skills: communication skills, organization skills, thinking skills, and time-management skills. It also promotes and fosters qualities such as insight, imagination, motivation, initiative, and self-discipline. These talents are useful, not only in school and university; they are life-skills of great relevance and wide application.

Tell me, I will forget
Show me, I may remember
Involve me, I will understand

Chinese proverb

RESEARCH

Selecting the Topic

Frequently, instructors will ask you to select your own topic. Being involved in the project from the outset confers a sense of ownership and invariably creates a heightened degree of engagement, commitment, and interest. Let us assume you are studying twentieth-century international history and your instructor has asked you to choose the topic for your term paper. After studying the course outline and surveying the textbook, you decide to select "Collective Security in the 1930s" as the broad topic you wish to investigate. We will use this topic as our example to illustrate the process of researching and writing a major essay or term paper. If you are allowed the freedom to select your own topic, be sure to choose one that interests you and offers you a challenge, but also one that is manageable in terms of its scope, complexity, and length.

Discuss your choice of topic with the instructor and clarify items such as the following:

- The number of sources to be used.
- Whether the sources should include both primary and secondary material.
- The citation or documentation procedures required.
- The length of the completed paper.

- The due date and whether there is a penalty for late submission.
- The overall structure, such as the nature of the introduction and the conclusion.
- Whether illustrations, such as statistical tables and graphs should be used.
- Matters of style, such as the use of the first person.
- Format and layout of the final copy.
- The criteria for assessment and whether a sample evaluation form is available.

Before starting your assignment, ensure that you understand precisely what is required and then consult your instructor regularly throughout the preparation of the essay. Since requirements may vary among instructors, you might consider making a copy of the above list — perhaps even adding your own ideas and questions — and checking off the various items during discussions with your instructor prior to beginning an assignment.

As soon as the due date is established, start planning a schedule for the completion of the various stages of the paper. Planning requires a practical process or pathway with clearly defined stages of development. Suggested stages for preparing a term paper or a major essay are outlined opposite and explained in the pages ahead. For example, you may wish to spend half the time on the research phase and the other half on the actual writing of the paper.

Alternatively, you may decide to spend about one third of the time on the preliminary research, one third on recording information, and one third on the actual writing. If the topic and the question have been assigned by the instructor some of the initial stages of the preliminary research will be eliminated and this will influence your scheduling.

Advance preparation is critical, since you are unlikely to learn much, derive any satisfaction, or achieve any success if your essay is written in frenzied haste the night before the assignment is due. **Effective planning depends on a systematic process for researching and writing your essay coupled with a careful allotment of time.**

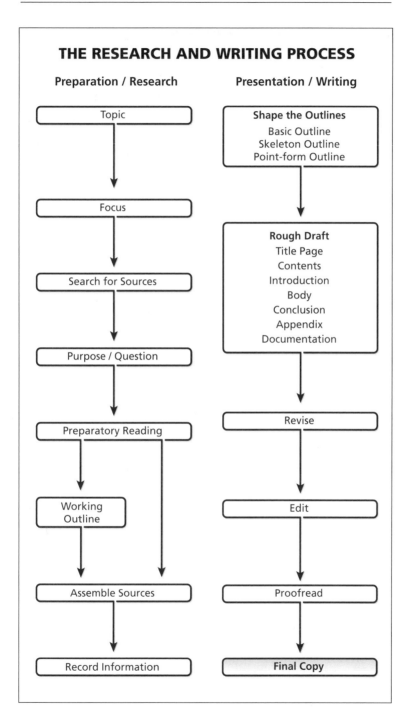

THE RESEARCH AND WRITING PROCESS

Preparation / Research

Presentation / Writing

Topic

Focus

Search for Sources

Purpose / Question

Preparatory Reading

Working Outline

Assemble Sources

Record Information

Shape the Outlines
Basic Outline
Skeleton Outline
Point-form Outline

Rough Draft
Title Page
Contents
Introduction
Body
Conclusion
Appendix
Documentation

Revise

Edit

Proofread

Final Copy

Narrowing the Focus

One of the major difficulties of essay writing is narrowing a broad topic to a specific focus. The failure to do so frequently results in a vague, superficial essay lacking depth, detail, and direction. **Fixing your focus on a specific and significant aspect of the topic is a crucial stage in preparing your essay.**

If the topic has been set by your instructor, certain constraints may be imposed on you. For example, not only may the topic be narrowed, but even the purpose or question may be spelled out, such as "Why did Australians volunteer to serve in the Anglo-Boer War in 1899?" However, if your instructor has not provided you with a specific issue or aspect, your first task is to narrow the topic and to isolate an important problem or a major controversy.

If you know very little about your topic, it will be necessary to do some preliminary reading to list potential issues for investigation. Textbooks, works from the course syllabus and the course bibliography, as well as general surveys, and reference books, such as encyclopedias, atlases, and dictionaries are useful for this exploratory reading. Not all dictionaries are language guides. For example, there are biographical dictionaries and historical dictionaries. The library catalogue and indexes at the back of books and encyclopedias may provide interesting leads. In addition, you might consult the *Library of Congress Subject Headings* and periodical and newspaper indexes which are explained in the Appendix. Viewing films and television documentaries on your topic could also suggest new ideas.

You can assemble a group of fellow students to brainstorm issues and exchange ideas about narrowing essay topics. As you read, think, discuss, and brainstorm, look for the major features, issues, and aspects of your topic that you think will provide an interesting and challenging focus for exploration and investigation. Jot these ideas down in a writing folder or a notebook or on a computer. It is a useful practice to keep a research log or an *Ideas and Questions*

Journal — an "*I.Q. Journal*" — in which to record ideas, questions and issues.   Instead of listing the issues and features in the conventional manner, you could also use a variety of diagrammatic techniques.

List or sketch as many possibilities in your *I.Q. Journal* as you can from your reading and brainstorming.   Reflect carefully on your list and circle the ones that interest you.   Then select **one** from your short-list.   It is important to devote your attention to an issue that is not too broad and not too narrow.   You should also avoid issues that lend themselves to a largely narrative, descriptive, or biographical approach. Controversial problems and contentious issues can work well because they are usually widely written about and vigorously debated.   They provide an opportunity to test conflicting perspectives and values, and enable you to leave your personal imprint on the completed essay.

Discuss your choice of focus with your instructor and obtain approval before continuing.   It is also a good idea to have one or two back up issues listed in your *I.Q. Journal,* in case you run into difficulties with your first choice. **Narrowing the topic is a crucial stage in the process because the issue, aspect, or feature that you select will provide the focus for your investigation**.

Frequently, this narrowing or focusing process will involve more than one stage.   If you had chosen "Collective Security in the 1930s" as your topic, you might decide to focus on the League of Nations.   You might then discover that the League is still too broad an aspect for investigation.   Further reading might lead you to examine the inability of the League of Nations to maintain international stability in the 1930s.

Imagine that your topic is a scene that you are viewing through a wide-angle zoom lens.[2]   You note all the important features in the field of vision and then you zoom in closer until a specific feature is clearly framed and focused.   All your attention will now be concentrated on this feature.   You can always zoom out again to check perspective and context.

Searching for Sources

Once you have decided on a specific focus for your essay, the next step is to compile a list of potential sources of information.* It is important to **determine as soon as possible whether there are sufficient sources available** on the issue that you intend to investigate. If not, you will have to substitute your second choice.

Libraries can appear overwhelming, but there is no need to panic. If introductory tours are available, start by signing up for a tour of your library and later wander around on your own, familiarizing yourself with the layout. Many libraries provide handouts on everything from regulations to lists of reference materials. Develop a collection of these information sheets and read them carefully. Approach the library staff if you have difficulties. They are the specialists with the expertise to answer your questions. Their advice and suggestions will save hours of your time.

A great variety of source material is available and most libraries have a wide array of searching techniques to trace this material. To avoid diverting you from the research process by describing these techniques in detail here, they have been placed in the Appendix. Read pages 107–113 carefully. Do not be intimidated by the range of research resources. You are likely to use only a few of these resources initially. As you undertake research assignments during your high school and university years, try to familiarize yourself with as many of these resources as possible. Test them out in your library: hands-on, practical experience is a far better teacher than a manual. Knowing which resources exist in your research field will not only save time but will allow you to build a wide-ranging list of sources. And, of course, a knowledge of the various research aids will make it easier for you to write subsequent essays and papers.

---

* You may wish to define the precise purpose of your essay before searching for sources. If so, merely reverse the next two stages, "Searching for Sources" and "Defining the Purpose" (pages 14–15).

As you work through the research aids, you will be searching for sources relevant to your issue — the focus of your assignment. This preliminary list of sources is known as your **Working Bibliography**. As you find relevant references, simply list the authors, titles, and publication details of the sources, as shown on the next page. There is no need to locate and assemble the material at this stage because you are primarily determining the availability of potential material, and you may not even have decided on the precise purpose of the essay yet. It is unlikely that someone will clean out the library holdings on your topic (unless the whole class is working on the same topic) because many sources are now in electronic form, and others, such as reference works and periodicals, may not leave the library. Furthermore, searching techniques have made a greater volume of source material available, so there is usually less pressure on limited library resources today.

Enter all the publication details for each source accurately because these details will be required for the final list of sources (Bibliography or Works Consulted). If you do this conscientiously, there will be no need to check the source details later and waste valuable time. Neither is there any need to write up these details in final format at this stage. However, if you wish to enter the details in a specific documentary style in your Working Bibliography, consult your instructor to determine the required style for the essay. You will notice in our examples on the following pages that we have used two different styles to illustrate how to set up a Working Bibliography. These styles are explained in detail on pages 63–100.

Although the entries in the final Bibliography or Works Consulted are listed alphabetically, do not attempt at this stage to place your preliminary sources in alphabetical order. Concentrate on building a diversified range of sources and list the relevant publication details accurately.

There are three recommended methods for building the Working Bibliography: you can use standard notepaper, index cards, or a computer. The bibliographic information can be listed in exactly the same way in all three methods, as demonstrated on the next three pages. Choose the method that best suits your needs.

Notepaper Method

As you discover potential sources of information, list them on standard notepaper and fill in all the essential bibliographic details as follows:

	Working Bibliography
LNLT	Northedge, F.S. *The League of Nations: Its Life and Times, 1920–1946.* Leicester: Leicester University Press, 1986. Public Library. JX 1975. N78.
CSPM	Egerton, George W. "Collective Security as Political Myth: Liberal Internationalism and the League of Nations in Politics and History." *International Historical Review,* 5 (1983): 496–524. University Library. SER: H1.15.
LN	"League of Nations." *Encyclopedia Britannica.* 1999. ‹http://www.britannica.com/bcom/eb/article/5/0, 5716,56405+1+55027,00.html› [16 Februrary 2001].

- Continue listing all your sources in this manner.
- The codes (e.g. "LNLT") represent shortened forms of the titles. Codes are used to identify sources during the research.
- Enter the library location and call number once you know where the source is held.

Index Card Method

As you discover potential sources of information, list them on separate index cards and fill in all the essential bibliographic details as follows:

> LNLT
>   Northedge, F.S. (1986). _The League_
>   _of Nations: Its life and times, 1920—1946._
>   Leicester: Leicester University Press.
>   Public Library, JX 1975. N78.

> CSPM
>   Egerton, George W. (1983). "Collective
>   security as political myth: Liberal
>   internationalism and the League of Nations
>   in politics and history." _International_
>   _Historical Review,_ 5: 496—524.
>   University Library. SER: H1.15.

- Continue listing all your sources in this manner.
- The codes (e.g. "LNLT") represent shortened forms of the titles. Codes are used to identify sources during the research.
- Enter the library location and call number once you know where the source is held

Computer Method

Computer technology is transforming researching techniques. You can use computers to search for sources, compile the Working Bibliography, and store the researched information. Using a computer and a modem, you can search library holdings and databases throughout the world. Electronic searching is explained on pages 107–108 in the Research Aids section of the Appendix. You can copy the sources manually from the screen onto index cards or notepaper, as illustrated on the previous two pages; alternatively, you can have the computer transfer the information to a Working Bibliography file and print it later.

You can also search manually for your sources in the various research aids in the library and then, using a portable computer and a word processing program, you can set up a Working Bibliography file and enter the publication details as shown on page 10. Software programs allow you to create your own electronic index cards, if you prefer cards to notepaper for your Working Bibliography.

❖ ❖ ❖

The range and calibre of your sources can dramatically enhance the quality of your essays. Refer to pages 114–117 to help you determine the calibre of your sources. When designing a search strategy for developing your Working Bibliography, try to balance books and articles, electronic and audio-visual information, old and new material, conservative and radical interpretations and primary and secondary sources. To expand the diversity of your sources you can classify them in groups, such as Books, Articles, Audio-Visual, Electronic and Primary. You can then use different coloured index cards, such as blue for books and yellow for articles, to identify the different categories of sources. Enter the details as shown on page 11. If you are using notepaper for your Working Bibliography, you can classify your sources in a similar way by devoting a separate page to each category. For example, head a page "Books," and then write in the details for each book, as shown on page 10.

If you are searching electronically, you can print your sources and cut and paste them onto coloured cards or pages of notepaper. Alternatively, you can copy the sources to disk instead of printing them. Then you can create separate files for the different categories, such as Books and Articles, and transfer the sources to the appropriate files. You can print them later if necessary. Whichever computer method you are using to search and list your sources, make sure to record exact addresses or use bookmarks so that you can locate the sources again.

You may wish to devise your own set of classified headings to extend the range of your sources. There is a rich vein of material available today and a variety of techniques to trace it. Combine tradition and technology with tenacity in combing the many resources. Careful use of these resources and frequent practice will save you hours of frustrated searching, and you will be surprised at the quantity of information you can assemble on almost any topic. You will undoubtedly experience obstacles in digging for material, but do not give up: the persistent researcher is invariably rewarded.

Once you have assured yourself that there are adequate sources available to develop your essay, move on to the next stage. The length of your Working Bibliography will be determined either by the nature of the assignment or by the instructor. For most high school and university papers, a preliminary list of eight to fifteen sources should be adequate. If, despite intensive searching, you find an insufficient number of sources, you will have to select another issue from the backup list in your *I.Q. Journal*. **Make the change at this early stage**. It is frustrating to discover as the deadline approaches that there are insufficient sources to build a paper. By determining the extent of potential sources at this stage of the process, you will avoid the agony of having to find another issue and start anew with the deadline looming.

Another advantage of developing the Working Bibliography in the early stages of the project is that interesting possibilities might emerge that may serve as the purpose of the essay. Abstracts, titles and subtitles of sources often suggest challenging research questions. Jot any interesting ideas down in your *I.Q. Journal.*

Defining the Purpose

Once you have narrowed your topic to an important issue or aspect and established that there are sufficient sources of information, the next step is to define more precisely the direction of your research. You can give a clear sense of direction to your essay by launching it with an incisive and challenging **research question**. This is a crucial stage because the question spells out your purpose — your quest is in the question. The research question also refines the focus and defines the scope of the essay. If you are expected to produce a short paper, do not get carried away and pose a question that would produce a book. If the question is clear and precise, it will give direction and purpose to the assignment. Your sole task is to answer the question. **The answer will form your thesis, argument or point of view**.

Since your goal is to present an argument, you should avoid questions that lead to biographical, narrative, or descriptive answers, such as "Who was Grey Owl?" or "What are the different types of Native Art?" Also, do not pose speculative or hypothetical questions, such as "Could Germany have won the Second World War?" There can be no conclusive answers to such conjectures. Avoid questions that may be based on unfounded assumptions, such as "Why was Lenin a successful leader?" The assumption here is that Lenin was a successful leader, and that might not turn out to be the consensus view of your sources. It would be safer to rephrase the question in an open-ended way as follows: "How successful was Lenin as a leader?"

Always try to formulate a **single**, challenging question that demands analysis and argument — a question that can be stated precisely and succinctly in just one sentence. Avoid compound or multiple questions because they invariably create confusion. "Why" questions such as "Why did the U.S.A. declare war in 1917?" work well because they lend themselves to clear, structured answers, and they usually avoid the biographical, narrative, or descriptive trap. In addition, they also give a well-defined focus and direction to your research.

Frequently, you will have discovered interesting ideas and questions while developing your Working Bibliography. Further brainstorming sessions with fellow students can help expand your range of options. If you still have difficulty in designing a good question, it may be necessary to do additional reading. Gather as many potential research questions as possible and list them in your *I.Q. Journal.* Think carefully before deciding on your first choice, and then check with the instructor to ensure that your research question is acceptable and appropriately phrased.

Let us return to our example, the inability of the League of Nations to maintain international stability in the 1930s. If our interest is in the diplomatic turmoil of the 1930s culminating in the outbreak of the Second World War in 1939, we might formulate the research question as follows: "Why did the League of Nations fail to maintain international stability in the 1930s?" The direction of the essay is clearly set. **Your task is to answer the question — that is the sole purpose of the assignment.**

There is an alternate method for launching your research. Some manuals suggest initiating the process of preparing an essay by proposing a thesis or tentative theory. But jumping from the broad topic to a statement of thesis or argument is a quantum leap that can be confusing and intimidating for many students. Another difficulty with this approach is that you must have the background knowledge to suggest a sound thesis or hypothesis as a starting point.* Launching your essay with a precise, open-ended question, such as "Why did the League of Nations fail to maintain international stability in the 1930s?" opens up a wider range of possibilities than starting from a fixed position, such as "The League of Nations failed because of ineffective leadership." It might be useful to remember Sherlock Holmes' advice: **never theorize in advance of the facts.**

---

* Certain types of assignments, especially those involving statistical data, do lend themselves to the formulation and testing of a hypothesis or a proposition. However, avoid starting your research with an "educated guess" and then selecting information "to prove the thesis." It is intellectual dishonesty to consciously select material to support a predetermined position, while ignoring information that contradicts to it.

Preparatory Reading

Once you have defined the purpose of your essay, you need to develop a better understanding of the focus of your investigation **before you start the detailed research**. In addition to reference works, such as encyclopedias that you may have consulted earlier, you might locate some of the shorter sources in your Working Bibliography and read them quickly. Pre-reading some of your sources will provide you with an overview of the content, and will also enable you to determine whether a particular source has any merit.

The preparatory reading is more focused and directed than the earlier exploratory and preliminary reading because you are now "preparing" yourself for an important stage of the research — recording information and ideas that you will need to develop your thesis or argument. The preparatory reading will provide you with the background knowledge needed to develop perceptive questions, and will help you judge what is relevant, reliable, and important in the answers. Much of the reading and brainstorming and even many of your research notes never appear in the final copy. But like the nine tenths of an iceberg that is below the surface of the water, they form the invisible foundations that keep the essay afloat.

While you are reading **keep the research question or purpose of the essay uppermost in your mind**. Elements of an argument or thesis might start to emerge. Likewise, a tentative structure for the essay might start to appear.* Note these responses and ideas in your *I.Q. Journal*. You might even discover a more interesting and challenging purpose than your original choice. Do not hesitate to change direction — providing the sources in your Working Bibliography are appropriate — and formulate another research question. Do it now, not later, but remember to discuss any changes with your instructor. Set aside time for the preparatory work in your scheduling **— the more time and effort expended initially in preparing the essay, the less is needed later in writing the essay.**

---

* If you prefer to use a Working Outline, see pages 118–122.

Recording Information and Ideas

Armed with a thorough understanding of the focus of your paper from your preparatory reading, a substantial list of sources, and an incisive question, you are now ready to start analyzing your material and recording the relevant information and ideas. **The preliminary research is essential: there are no shortcuts to success**.

First, you have to locate and assemble your sources. Do not panic if you cannot find all the sources listed in your Working Bibliography, as it is unlikely that they will all be available in your community libraries. That is why you originally listed more sources than you really needed. The number of sources that you actually use may be determined by the instructor, by the scope of the essay, or by the length of the sources themselves. You should be able to complete a high school or a university paper with between five and ten sources. As you track down a source, note the library location and catalogue number (if you have not done so already) in your Working Bibliography so that you can find it again easily if necessary.

Using a variety of source material will improve your essay. A source may be biased, unbalanced, or even erroneous. By consulting a number of sources, you gain access to a wider range of interpretations and information. Frequently you will encounter conflicting information, and a wider range of sources will often enable you to confirm (or reject) controversial information. To avoid diverting you from the explanation of the research process in this section, the nature, use, and evaluation of sources have been placed in the Appendix. Read pages 114–117 carefully once you are comfortable with the research process.

Remember that your task is to develop a thoughtful and convincing answer to your research question. Since you cannot remember everything you read, a systematic method of recording ideas and information is essential. **It is impossible to develop a good essay without an organized collection of notes**. It is worth remembering the Chinese proverb that the palest ink is better than the most retentive memory.

Research involves analyzing, selecting, and recording information and ideas. Analysis means breaking something down into its smaller elements. Analysis involves a careful examination and dissection of your material and the identification and isolation of details and ideas in accordance with the purpose of your assignment. As you read through your sources, examine the material carefully and extract the important ideas and information (the "smaller elements") that are relevant to your research question. Once you have selected the relevant details and ideas, record them in your research notes. **The research question guides your research**. The question directs the analysis, the selection, and the recording of the evidence.

Research in the humanities is not a mechanical gathering of "facts." It is a complex process requiring both critical thought and creative imagination. Read critically: do not accept ideas and interpretations blindly. Be skeptical: read between the lines and beyond the print. Question continuously as you read and examine carefully the arguments of the authors. Raise your own stimulating and challenging questions; they can yield surprising new insights.

Take special care in the way you select information and ideas to record in your notes — to look for information just to "prove" a preconceived position or thesis is biased research. Biased research is both suspect and unethical. You should consider all perspectives and approaches to your question and **record all relevant information**, whether they support or contradict your personal position on the issue that you are investigating.

There are four main types of notes:

- Direct quotations.
- Personal insights, comments, and questions.
- Paraphrasing information and ideas.
- Summarizing information and ideas.

Reading, analyzing, selecting, and recording the evidence that you will need to develop your point of view or thesis is a major part of preparing research papers. Allow at least **one third** of the overall time that you have set aside to produce your paper for this important stage.

Itemized below are some suggestions to assist you in compiling your research notes:

- Try to pre-read your sources and then reread them and record your notes.

- Be concise, clear, and accurate.

- Use the table of contents and index in each book so that you can save time by focusing on the relevant pages only.

- Add your own ideas, comments, and questions; do not just quote, summarize, or paraphrase.

- If you develop your own shorthand system for recording notes, ensure that your abbreviations and symbols will make sense to you later.

- Use your own words where possible.

- Restrict the number of direct quotations.

- Transcribe direct quotations carefully, enclosing them in quotation marks.

- Record all the essential information so that you do not have to consult your sources again when composing the essay.

- Indicate whether a piece of evidence is established fact or subjective opinion.

- Material may be interesting and it may true, but ask yourself if it is relevant to your question or purpose.

- Plagiarism is the unacknowledged use of someone else's ideas. Identifying the sources of all your notes can help you avoid charges of plagiarism.

- If you find new sources, add them to your Working Bibliography.

- Make comments on the merits of each source once you have used it.

You can use index cards, standard notepaper, or a computer to record information and ideas. The notemaking techniques for index cards and notepaper are described separately in the pages ahead so that they can be read independently.

Notepaper Method

Set up your notepaper recording system by ruling a right-hand margin of 2–3 cm **on the front side of the page only**. Prepare a number of pages in advance so that you have a supply of notepaper for your research notes.

If you were doing the League of Nations essay, you would take one of your available sources, for example, *The League of Nations: Its Life and Times, 1920–1946* by F.S. Northedge, and start looking specifically for information relevant to the research question. On page 52 of the book there is reference to the limited power of the League. Since this point is relevant to your question, you would record it as a summary note in the centre column of your notepaper, as shown in our example on the following page.

You must identify the source of the note in case you need to refer to it for further details or you need to acknowledge the source in a documentary note later. It is not necessary to record all the publication details (author, title, publisher, year) again for each note. Simply use the code which represents a shortened form of the title as explained on page 10. For example, "LNLT" stands for *The League of Nations: Its Life and Times, 1920–1946*. In addition to the source, you must also indicate the page reference for the information. Therefore, "LNLT 52" indicates that the information is from page 52 in *The League of Nations: Its Life and Times, 1920–1946,* as illustrated opposite.

Reflect on what you have done:
- You have discovered relevant information pertaining to the research question.
- You have recorded it in note form.
- You have indicated the source and page number.

The whole process of recording the ideas and information needed to develop your thesis is encapsulated in these three elements above. But remember that the process is underpinned by continuous probing and questioning and by constant examination and dissection of your material.

Following the suggestions on page 19, continue reading through LNLT looking for information and ideas relevant to

LNLT	*League had limited power; decisions were recommendations and not binding on members (except when member states were at war).*
52	
LNLT	*No authority from above; co-operation from below and an aversion to force seemed to be the approach.*
69	
LNLT	*"That the League lived, flourished, and died within three months during the Abyssinian crisis is sufficient proof, of course, that its fatal weakness did not lie in the failings of its chief defenders, Britain and France, but in deeper faults which had lain there from the beginning."*
276	

Source code and page — **Note or quotation**

the research question. On page 69, there is reference to the authority of the League. In similar fashion to the first note, you record the information in the centre column and identify the source by its code and page number in the left-hand margin. Nothing is written in the right-hand margin at this stage. Leave a line between each note so that the notes can be separated later.

On page 276 of LNLT there is mention of the Abyssinian crisis, and you decide to record the information verbatim in case it is needed as a quotation. Transcribe it accurately and use quotation marks to indicate that it is a quotation and not a summary or a paraphrased note. The source code and page reference are recorded as explained.

Work through your first source questioning, analyzing, selecting, and recording the relevant information. Do not record information just because it is "interesting." **Does the information help answer the research question?** That must always be your criterion. Once you have filled your first page of notepaper, continue on another page. Do not write on the reverse side of the page because it will be impossible to separate individual notes later during the outlining process.

When you have completed your first source, check it off in your Working Bibliography and move on to the next source — George Egerton's article, coded "CSPM", for example. It is not necessary to start a new page of notepaper for each source. On page 513 of article CSPM, you find mention of the nature of support for collective security, and you summarize the point in your notes and identify the source, as shown below. Read through the source isolating the relevant information and recording it as described.

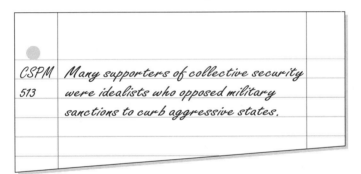

Continue reading all your available sources, searching for information, ideas, and insights relevant to your purpose or question and systematically record the details and identify the sources on your notepaper.

While you are engaged in your research, you may discover so much information on one aspect that you decide to narrow the focus even further and zoom in closer. For example, you may decide to focus only on the League's role in the Abyssinian crisis. You may even decide on a minor shift of direction and modify your question slightly during the course of the research. **Always consult your instructor before making any changes.**

Index Card Method

You have a choice of three common sizes of index cards. Since each note should be written on a separate card, it is recommended that you use **the smallest size of index card.**

If you were doing the League of Nations essay, you would take one of your available sources, for example, *The League of Nations: Its Life and Times, 1920-1946* by F.S. Northedge, and start looking specifically for information relevant to the research question. On page 52 of the book there is reference to the limited power of the League. Since this point is relevant to your question, you would record it as a summary note on an index card, as shown below.

You must identify the source of the note in case you need to refer to it for further details or you need to acknowledge the source in a reference or documentary note later. It is not necessary to write out all the publication details (author, title, publisher, year) again for each note. Simply use the code which represents a shortened form of the title, as explained on page 10. For example, "LNLT" stands for *The League of Nations: Its Life and Times, 1920-1946.* In addition to the source, you must also indicate the page reference for the information. Therefore, "LNLT 52" indicates that the information is from page 52 in *The League of Nations: Its Life and Times, 1920-1946,* as illustrated below.

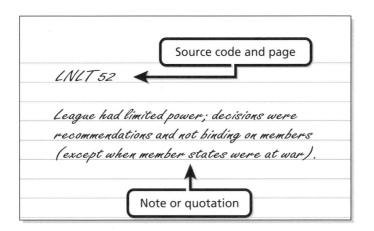

Reflect on what you have done:

- You have discovered relevant information pertaining to the research question.
- You have recorded it in note form.
- You have indicated the source and page number.

The whole process of recording the ideas and information needed to develop your thesis is encapsulated in these three elements above. But the process is underpinned by continuous probing and questioning and by constant examination and dissection of your material.

Following the suggestions on page 19, continue reading through LNLT looking for information and ideas relevant to the research question. On page 69, there is reference to the authority of the League. In similar fashion to the first note, you record the information on a separate index card and identify the source by its code and page number in the left-hand corner, as shown below.

> *LNLT 69*
>
> *No authority from above; co-operation from below and an aversion to force seemed to be the approach.*

On page 276 of LNLT there is mention of the Abyssinian crisis, and you decide to record the information verbatim in case it is needed as a quotation. Transcribe it accurately and use quotation marks to indicate that it is a quotation and not a summary or a paraphrased note. The source code and page reference are recorded as explained earlier. You may wish to make a comment about the quotation on the reverse side of the card.

> *LNLT 276*
>
> *"That the League lived, flourished, and died within three months during the Abyssinian crisis is sufficient proof, of course, that its fatal weakness did not lie in the failings of its chief defenders, Britain and France, but in deeper faults which had lain there from the beginning."*

Work through your first source questioning, analyzing, selecting, and recording the relevant information. Do not record information just because it is "interesting." **Does the information help answer the research question?** That must always be your criterion.

When you have completed your first source, check it off in your Working Bibliography and move on to the next available source — George Egerton's article, coded "CSPM", for example.   On page 513 of article CSPM, you find mention of the nature of support for collective security, and you summarize the point on a card and identify the source, as shown below.

> *CSPM 513*
>
> *Many supporters of collective security were idealists who opposed military sanctions to curb aggressive states.*

On the next page of article CSPM, you read about declining support for the League and you record the point as a quotation.

CSPM 514

British public support for the League was "cast adrift as the government attempted to cover the tracks of its duplicity and confusion, following the path of appeasement and gradual rearmament."

Continue consulting all your available sources — whether they are primary or secondary, oral or online — searching for information, ideas, and insights relevant to your purpose or question and then systematically record the details and identify the sources on your cards.

While you are engaged in your research, you may discover so much information on one aspect that you decide to narrow the focus even further and zoom in closer. For example, you may decide to focus only on the League's role in the Abyssinian crisis. You may even decide on a minor shift of direction and modify your question slightly during the course of the research. **Always consult your instructor before making any changes.**

❖ ❖ ❖

By comparing the notepaper notes on page 21 and 22 with the index card notes above, you will notice that the only difference between the two methods is that the notepaper method links the "index cards" together. Later, when the notepaper notes are separated, the difference disappears. Choose the method that best suits your needs.

Bear these points in mind when you are using index cards:

- Do not confuse bibliographic cards (page 11), which list sources, with note cards (page 23), which contain ideas and information.

- Each note card should contain two items:

  1. Source code and page

  2. Note

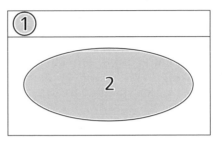

- Write just one note on each card.

- Use the smallest index cards. It is easier to shape your outlines with small cards, each containing just one major point.

- Your research cards have no special order, and as they are all independent, there is no need to number them.

- Finish writing a long note on the reverse side of the card rather than continuing on another card.

- Duplicate diagrams, graphs, and statistical tables and paste them on cards.

- Keep separate "date cards" while researching history essays to facilitate creating a chronology or time-line.

- Use your initials as the source code when recording personal ideas and comments.

- You may also use coloured cards to distinguish different types of cards. For example, you might use white cards for research notes, blue cards for sources, and yellow cards as "date cards." (If you colour-coded your Working Bibliography cards, as explained on page 12, do not use coloured cards, as suggested here.)

- Once you have finished using a source, write critical comments on the reverse side of the bibliographic cards. These comments can be used to compile an annotated bibliography for your essay.

- Use a file box or two-ring card folder to hold your cards.

Computer Method

Recording your ideas and information with a computer is also an option. If you prefer using a computer, you should still read pages 20–27 carefully because the notemaking techniques for notepaper and index cards also apply to computer usage. If you prefer the notepaper method, you can set up a word processor file for your notes. If you prefer index cards, there are software packages that will allow you to write, edit, retrieve, and sort "cards" on the screen. Record the details, identify the sources, and follow the procedures described earlier.

Modems and networks are providing quick and easy access to library holdings and other databases. The information in these databases is often in a variety of formats, such as text, video, sound, graphics, and photographs. You can browse and import information in text or graphic form directly to your note files, but remember the **warning about plagiarism** when downloading.

Remember to keep these points in mind:

- Allow enough time in your schedule for preparing your essay. You need adequate time to read, research, respond, reflect, and record.

- The research question directs the analysis, the selection, and the recording process.

- A comprehensive and organized system of notes is essential. It is exceedingly difficult to write an intelligent essay without good notes.

- The process described is not a rigid straightjacket; it is flexible. Modify it and shape a research pathway to suit your needs.

- Think and question continuously as you research, and use your *I.Q. Journal* or your notes to list ideas and insights. **Your questions may be more important than the answers.**

- There is a time to stop digging and start shaping.[3] Learn to impose limits on your research.

PRESENTATION

Introduction

Now that the analysis and the recording have been completed, you can start shaping and composing your answer to the research question. The analysis is one side of the process, the synthesis is the other side. Your answer represents **your argument, point of view, or thesis** — it is the axis on which the essay revolves.

Composing the answer is a crucial phase, because the success of your essay hinges on your ability to communicate your ideas clearly to the reader. Clarity of argument is largely dependent upon **the style and the structure** of your essay. Contrary to what many people think, structure does not suppress creativity; it promotes clear, creative expression.[4] The ABC formula below is a simple and effective model for structuring an essay or term paper. Style is the mortar that will hold it together.

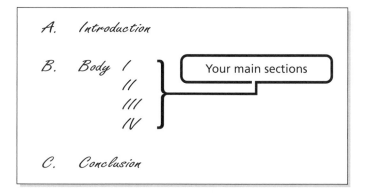

Shaping the Outlines

Once you have completed your reading and recording, your notes will be organized on index cards, notepaper or computer. It is impossible to write a final copy straight from these notes. A number of intermediate stages are necessary to ensure quality. Shaping the structure of the essay is your next task. The following section on outlining demonstrates the importance of organization in developing clarity of argument **before** you start to draft your essay.

The first step is to create an outline that imposes order on your notes and ideas. The method in this manual describes what might be called "conventional outlining." Some students might have alternative organizing systems, such as diagrammatic techniques. The nature of your system does not matter, **what is important is that you have an organizing system**.

Before creating your detailed outlines, you should read ahead about the roles of the introduction, body and conclusion on pages 42–50. You should also read about the use of quotations on pages 59–62 and the matter of opposing viewpoints on page 40. All these features and details will have to be included in your outlines.

Basic Outline

Allow yourself **time** to reread your notes and to reflect on the ideas in your *I.Q. Journal* while keeping the research question uppermost in your mind. Try to isolate the main factors around which you can structure an answer in the body of the essay. You may even have a tentative list of possible factors that you jotted down in your *I.Q. Journal* during the course of the preparatory reading and the research. We have isolated three main factors around which to develop our answer to the question, "Why did the League of Nations fail to maintain international stability in the 1930s?" This list of main factors is called the **Basic Outline,** as shown on the top of the next page.

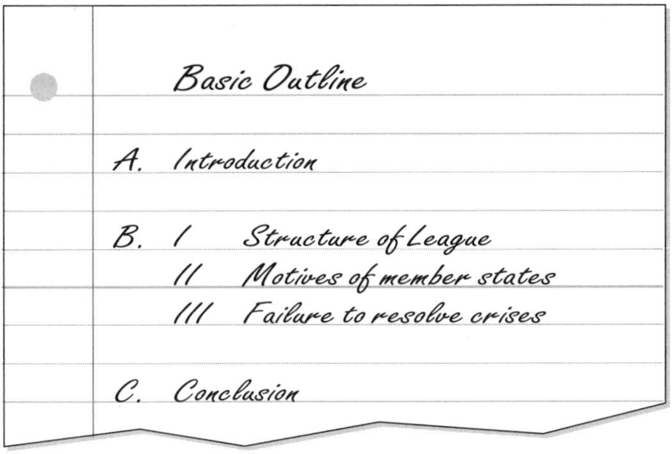

Basic Outline

A. Introduction

B. I   Structure of League
    II   Motives of member states
    III Failure to resolve crises

C. Conclusion

If you used notepaper for recording your information, separate the individual notes with scissors (that is why you wrote on one side of the page only), in effect making "cards" out of them, as shown below.

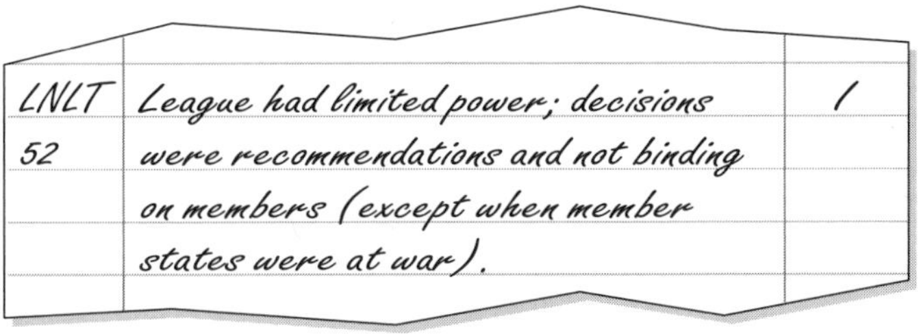

| LNLT 52 | League had limited power; decisions were recommendations and not binding on members (except when member states were at war). | I |

Read through the separated notepaper slips carefully and group them according to the sections of the Basic Outline. The next step is to number the notepaper slips according to the sections of the Basic Outline into which they fall. Use the empty right-hand column to indicate the numbered section of the Basic Outline, as shown above. For instance, all notes dealing with problems associated with the structure of the League of Nations are labeled I because "Structure of the League" is section I of the Basic Outline, as shown at the top of the page. It is a good idea to use paper clips to group the notepaper slips.

If you used index cards for recording your information, go through your cards in exactly the same way and group and number them according to the sections of the Basic Outline. Use the upper right-hand corner of each card for the section number. Arrange your cards in their groups in a file box, a two-ring card folder, or use rubber bands to group them.

LNLT 52   *1*

League had limited power; decisions were recommendations and not binding on members (except when member states were at war).

Some notes will not fit into the major sections of the body or in the introduction and they will have to be discarded. Do not be concerned if you cannot use all your notes. The rejected notes are not wasted: they are part of the "invisible foundations" that support the one tenth of the iceberg above the water — your essay.

If you used a computer to record your information, you might find it easier at this stage to print copies of your notes and organize them manually, as described above. If you used "electronic notepaper," you can create separate files for each section of the Basic Outline, and then transfer the individual notes to the appropriate files. If you used index card software, sort and group your "electronic cards", as explained above.

There is no magic number of body sections in a Basic Outline — from three to six will handle most questions. But **ensure that all sections address the research question**. The basic structure of the essay is now in place, although it is possible that the actual order of the body sections may change later during the drafting stage.

Skeleton Outline

The Basic Outline provides the overall structure of your essay. To move from the Basic Outline to the more detailed Skeleton Outline, read carefully through the notes of each section of the Basic Outline, identifying the important subsections. The advantage of index cards or notepaper strips is that you can take a section at a time and spread the strips or cards on a table, move them around, and then map out the substructure for each section. This stage, containing the main sections with their subsections, is called the Skeleton Outline.

Skeleton Outline

A. Introduction
   1. Background
   2. Focus/Problem
   3. Question/Purpose
   4. Range of viewpoints
   5. Thesis

B. I Structure of League
   1. Limits to power
   2. Problem with mandate
   3. Abuse of major powers

   II Motives of member states
   1. Lack of idealism
   2. "Balance of power" diplomacy
   3. Nationalistic ends and propaganda

   III Failure to resolve crises
   1. Manchuria (powerlessness)
   2. Abyssinia (secret diplomacy)
   3. Loss of public confidence
   4. Inequality of member states

C. Conclusion

Point-form Outline

Once you have mapped out the substructure of the Skeleton Outline, you need to isolate the supporting details for your argument. This should not be a lengthy process because you have a structure in place, a clear idea of the direction your essay is taking, and a good overall knowledge of the contents of your notes. To include every detail unearthed during the research will overwhelm the reader and destroy the clarity of your answer; therefore, further selection is necessary. Read through your notes, carefully selecting only what is essential to your argument. Although you may wish to use all your hard-earned notes, you must be ruthless and retain only the relevant details. The supporting details are arranged under the structure of the Basic and the Skeleton Outlines, as shown on the following pages. This stage is known as the Point-form Outline.

Remember that **the aim of your essay is to develop an answer to your research question and to articulate it in the form of an argument or thesis.** In our example, we are not simply describing or chronicling the failure of The League of Nations — we are explaining why we believe it failed to maintain international security.

Judgments, interpretations, and opinions have to be supported by relevant evidence and developed through sound reasoning if your argument is to be credible and convincing. Your supporting evidence will come in many forms: statistics, cases, examples, and quotations, both from primary sources and authorities. To fashion a successful essay requires the fusing of your supporting evidence with insight, reason, and logic.

But your responsibility is also to produce a balanced presentation of your point of view and an unbiased response to the research question. You must not "stack the deck" by consciously selecting material to promote a preconceived position. **Consciously promoting a preconceived position is bias.** In addition to practical matters, such as structure, there are philosophical issues, such as selection, subjectivity, and bias that have to be addressed as you construct your outlines. Read page 38 carefully before you proceed with your Point-form Outline.

Use as few words as possible in the Point-form Outline; do not rewrite your notes.   You can always refer to your research notes to check details when writing the rough draft. Since the order of the body sections may change during the drafting, it is advisable to **devote a separate page** of notepaper to each major section in the Point-form Outline, as shown below and on the next page.   Rearranging the sections in the preferred order when preparing the rough draft will then be easy.

We have taken the introduction, shown below, and section III of the body, shown overleaf, to illustrate the organization of the Point-form Outline.

Point-form Outline

A. *Introduction*

1. *Background*
   - *conceived during WWI*
   - *Covenant in peace treaties*
   - *objectives*

2. *Focus/Problem*
   - *not new*
   - *CofV and UN*
   - *short peace*

3. *Question/Purpose*
   - *why did LofN fail to maintain intl. stability?*

4. *Range of viewpoints*
   - *charter flawed*
   - *inclusion in treaties*
   - *absence of US*
   - *lack of commitment*
   - *structure*
   - *major crises*

5. *Thesis*
   - *3 main factors (structure, motives, crises)*

B. III Failure to resolve crises

1. Manchuria (powerlessness)
  – Western policy of non-recognition
  – unwilling to use force against Japan
  – Japan leaves League

2. Abyssinia (secret diplomacy)
  – need for Italian support
  – reluctance to impose oil embargo
  – Hoare-Laval plan

3. Loss of public confidence
  – peace ballot shows support
  – disillusionment after Hoare-Laval

4. Inequality of member states
  – lack of racial equality clause
  – League primarily serving Europe

If you have been using a computer, look through your electronic notes, isolating the subsections of the Skeleton Outline and the supporting details of the Point-form Outline. Most word processors allow you to open more than one document window at a time, enabling you to develop your outline in one window while viewing your notes in the other. Most word processing programs also have an Outline function. This function will automatically number the sections and subsections as you go along, making it easy for you to create outlines. Once you have composed your outlines on the computer, print copies so that you can review and revise them.

Developing the three outlines is not excessively time-consuming. The outlines will enable you to determine if there are any weak spots in the argument. For instance, a Point-form Outline might show you that one of your main sections contains insufficient material to support your thesis, and that it might be better to merge it with another section or eliminate it. Furthermore, the outlines will expedite drafting your essay. **"Writer's block" is rarely a problem if you are in control of your material before attempting to draft your essay.**

We have taken B. III from the previous page and shown how it expands at each outline stage in the diagram below. Clarity of argument is a function of both style and structure. In shaping your outlines you will have created the structure. Style is the mortar that will hold the essay together and enhance both the clarity and the impact of the argument.

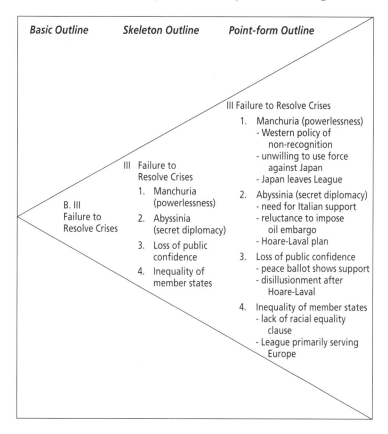

Basic Outline   *Skeleton Outline*   *Point-form Outline*

B. III
Failure to
Resolve Crises

III Failure to
     Resolve Crises
  1. Manchuria
      (powerlessness)
  2. Abyssinia
      (secret diplomacy)
  3. Loss of public
      confidence
  4. Inequality of
      member states

III Failure to Resolve Crises
  1. Manchuria (powerlessness)
      - Western policy of
        non-recognition
      - unwilling to use force
        against Japan
      - Japan leaves League
  2. Abyssinia (secret diplomacy)
      - need for Italian support
      - reluctance to impose
        oil embargo
      - Hoare-Laval plan
  3. Loss of public confidence
      - peace ballot shows support
      - disillusionment after
        Hoare-Laval
  4. Inequality of member states
      - lack of racial equality
        clause
      - League primarily serving
        Europe

Subjectivity, Selection and Bias.

The entire process of researching and then composing an essay is influenced by our unique view of the world. This subjective worldview has been to a great extent shaped by our life experiences. We view both the past and the present through the prism of these experiences. Family, friends, institutions, and the values of society have all left their imprint. This process of socialization or cultural conditioning influences the selection of our subject, the nature of the questions we ask, the manner in which we filter our information, and the methods we use to develop our answers.[5] Much as we may try to be "objective," subjectivity and relativity are inescapable in the social sciences and the humanities.

The selection process, an integral aspect of preparing an essay, is also affected by our subjective perspective. In selecting and narrowing the topic, and developing a Working Bibliography, you had to make choices. You chose the most relevant sources from your Working Bibliography on which to make your notes. You further selected from these notes to compose your outlines. Since you are developing a personal point of view that is shaped and supported by selected evidence, you must be meticulous in the way you evaluate your sources and impartial in the selection of your supporting evidence.

We cannot escape our subjective nature and it may be difficult to remain impartial on some emotionally charged issues, but we must strive at all times to be fair and honest researchers and writers. That means we must avoid bias. Bias is a consciously partisan selection of information to promote a preconceived point of view.[6] Bias is prejudging an issue, and that is prejudice. **Bias is unethical and unacceptable.   Subjectivity is innate and unavoidable.**

Since subjective selection is such an integral feature of humanities and social science research, consensus is rare in the study of human affairs. You will encounter a range of equally valid opinions and theories amongst authorities and even among your peers. Likewise, there is no final proof and no ultimate truth — most conclusions and interpretations in the humanities and social sciences are tentative at best.

The Rough Draft

Do not attempt to write your final copy straight from your Point-form Outline. It is essential to allow time in your schedule so that you can prepare a rough draft first. Roughing out the **complete** essay in a preliminary draft and laying it out in the required format will enhance the final copy significantly. If you use a computer to prepare your rough draft, producing the final copy will be a quick and painless process.

There are a number of conventions of essay writing that must be incorporated in your rough draft. Some are described in this section while others are explained later in the manual. Read the references to the following items carefully **before** commencing the rough draft. Although you may have discussed some of these items at the outset of the assignment, confirm your instructor's preferences before proceeding with the rough draft.

- Length

- Method of documentation

- Use of quotations

- Opposing viewpoints

- Overall structure

- Subjectivity and bias

- Style and expression

- Paragraphing

- Illustrations

- Appendix

- Abstract

- Title page

- Table of contents

- Final copy format

Once you have completed the Point-form Outline, most of the hard work is over. If you have arranged the sections of the Point-form Outline on separate pages, it is now easy to rearrange them in a more appropriate order. Having worked extensively on the detailed outlines, you should have a clear idea of the relative importance of each section. Normally an **ascending order of interest and importance** is the most effective way of developing your thesis.

Once you have finalized the order of the main sections, the shape of your paper will have emerged. It is a relatively easy task to start fleshing the essay out and weaving it together in a rough draft now that you have a detailed structure in place. All the work that went into preparing the outlines will start to pay off. Another advantage is that the detailed outlines provide a formula for developing your paragraphs, as explained on pages 46–49. With your course clearly mapped out, a detailed structure in place, and a clear grasp of the main features, your essay will progress under its own momentum.

One of the matters that you have to consider (and discuss with your instructor) is whether you should address arguments and ideas that run counter to your thesis, or whether you should ignore opposing viewpoints. In shorter papers you will probably not have the space, but in longer research assignments by challenging counter arguments you will lend an enhanced credibility to your thesis. Rebuttals should be inserted where they fit most naturally into the overall structure of the essay, and they must be included in planning the detailed outlines. You can refute contradictory viewpoints immediately after the thesis statement, or at appropriate places as you develop and substantiate your thesis. Alternatively, you may address other points of view in footnotes or endnotes.

How long should the essay be? This is one of the most common questions raised by students. In many cases your instructor will determine the length of the paper and you should never exceed that length by more than ten per cent. If no word limit is set, the length will be established by the demands of the question and your response to it. Shorter rather than longer is a sound rule to follow. **Remember that your words should be weighed, not counted.**

If you are using a computer, you should take advantage of the fact that most word processors allow you to work on two documents simultaneously, usually by splitting the screen into two windows as shown below. Bring up your outline in one window and begin writing the essay in the other window. You can switch back and forth easily. You can also bring up the files that serve as your electronic notes in one window and transfer relevant information from that window into the window where you are writing the draft by cutting and pasting. But use this feature sparingly because an essay constructed by mindlessly stringing together your research notes will not make any sense to your readers.

Once you have completed the rough draft you can work on the essay in fullscreen mode. You may find it useful to increase the line spacing and widen the margins when printing a draft copy so that you will have more white space for revising and editing. Do not forget to remove the extra space before printing the final copy. A printed copy will also provide a backup in the event of a major malfunctioning of your computer.

WORD PROCESSOR   ▫▫▫

File   Edit   View   Format   Window   Help

B. III Failure to resolve crises
1. Manchuria (powerlessness)
   - Western policy of non-recognition
   - unwilling to use force against Japan
   - Japan leaves League

2. Abyssinia (secret diplomacy)
   - need for Italian support
   - reluctance to impose oil embargo
   - Hoare-Laval plan

3. Loss of public confidence
   - peace ballot shows support
   - disillusionment after Hoare-Laval

4. Inequality of member states
   - lack of racial equality clause
   - League primarily serving Europe

1935 was, like Manchuria, a clear case of aggression by one member against another. Britain and France were not prepared to risk their relations with Italy at a time when Nazi Germany increasingly appeared to threaten European security. While they were prepared to condemn Mussolini's aggression against Abyssinia, Britain and France refused to take decisive action and impose an oil embargo. Worse still, Britain and France, in secret negotiations outside the forum of the League, were attempting to placate Italy. When the Hoare-Laval Plan which granted parts of Abyssinia to Italy was exposed, it also revealed the duplicitous nature of Franco-British policy. The Abyssinian crisis was a decisive event in the decline of

Drafting the Introduction

The introduction should prepare the reader by providing the background, such as setting the historical context, and by establishing the direction of the essay. Although usually short, introductions are important because they set the general tone of your work and because first impressions can influence the reader. Since essays and term papers are scholarly studies, it is inappropriate to inject humour and sensationalism into the introduction to "grab" the reader's attention. Try to "introduce" the reader to your essay in a more serious and formal, yet nevertheless interesting manner. If you have followed a systematic research and outlining process, you should have no difficulty in drafting the introduction first. Do not leave the introduction until last, almost as an afterthought.

The "coffee filter" model offers a practical framework for an introduction for a major term paper or an extended essay.

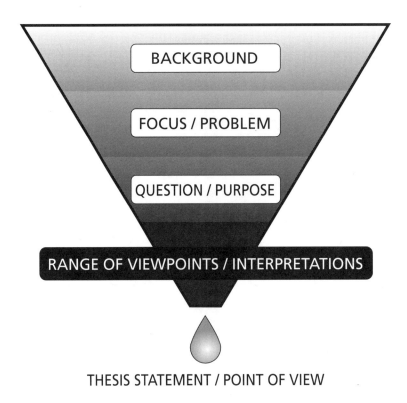

BACKGROUND

FOCUS / PROBLEM

QUESTION / PURPOSE

RANGE OF VIEWPOINTS / INTERPRETATIONS

THESIS STATEMENT / POINT OF VIEW

The coffee filter formula prepares the reader by first presenting relevant **background** information which will be largely descriptive, narrative, or biographical. Next explain the **focus** of the essay and its importance as a field of study. Then you should indicate the **purpose** of your essay — to provide the reader with a signpost showing the direction of your assignment. Stating your research question is probably the clearest means of expressing the purpose of the essay. If you find it difficult to integrate a question smoothly into the text of the introduction, try stating the objective of the assignment in a more traditional way, such as "The purpose of this paper is to explain why the League of Nations failed to maintain international stability in the 1930s."

The next step is to indicate the **range of viewpoints** and the nature of the intellectual debate surrounding your issue. If differing opinions do not exist, then simply omit this section in the introduction. In this case, the coffee filter changes its shape to that of a funnel, as shown below.[7]

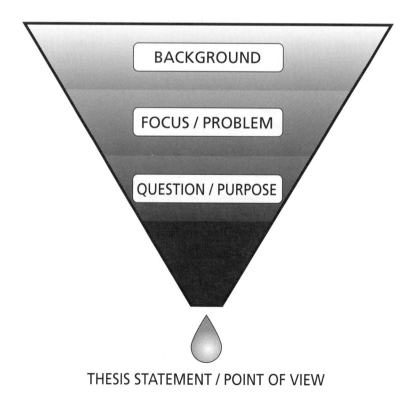

BACKGROUND

FOCUS / PROBLEM

QUESTION / PURPOSE

THESIS STATEMENT / POINT OF VIEW

Finally, state your argument or **thesis** (answer to your question) clearly. It is important to inform the readers of your position or point of view before you start developing it in the body of your essay. Academic papers are not detective thrillers aimed at keeping the reader in suspense until the final paragraph. Check with your instructor before using the first person in the thesis statement. Many instructors discourage the use of "I" in an essay. Check also the preferred length of the thesis statement with your instructor. Should it be a concise one or two sentence assertion or should it be an expanded explanation with details of the argument? Some instructors even recommend a description of the structure of the essay as part of an expanded thesis statement.

Despite its brevity, the introduction is an important and integral part of your essay. It will probably vary from about ten to fifteen percent of the overall length of the essay, but it must never overwhelm and overshadow the development of your argument in the body of the essay. Check the details of the introduction carefully with your instructor, because some instructors may only require short introductions of one or two paragraphs. Definitions tend to interrupt the flow of the introduction. It is advisable to place them in footnotes or endnotes. No matter the length or the nature of the introduction, remember to mention the three P's — the **problem**, the **purpose**, and your **point of view**.

On the opposite page, you will find the introduction to the League of Nations essay. It is shown here in final form after revising and editing. We have used a subheading for illustrative purposes only; many instructors discourage subheadings, especially in shorter essays.

The detailed outlines offer a formula for developing your paragraphs. The coffee filter or funnel components, which are simply the subsections of the Skeleton Outline (page 33), provide the paragraph structure for the introduction. The Point-form Outline (page 35) supplies the supporting details. Both the filter and the funnel are flexible models for shaping the paragraph structure and you will notice in our example opposite that we have combined the focus and the question in one paragraph.

Introduction

The League of Nations was conceived during the carnage of the First World War. In an attempt to prevent the re-occurrence of an international tragedy of this scale, the peacemakers included the Covenant of the League in the peace treaties that concluded the war. The League had two main objectives: to promote peace by the collective collaboration of member states against an aggressor and to improve social and economic conditions worldwide.

The attempt to establish an international organization to maintain peace and balance power relationships among members was not new. The Congress of Vienna had been formed after the Napoleonic Wars and brought peace to Europe for many decades. Likewise, the United Nations, successor to the League of Nations, has had relative success in avoiding major conflagrations. Yet within two decades of the formation of the League, Europe embarked on a bloody war that eventually engulfed most of the world. The tragically short period of peace raises the question why the League of Nations failed to maintain international stability in the 1930s.

Writers have suggested many reasons. The founding charter, the Covenant, was not only flawed, but its inclusion in the peace treaties caused resentment among the defeated powers. The absence of the United States as a member and the lack of commitment by major powers such as Germany, the USSR, Italy, and Japan relegated the burden of bolstering the League to Britain and France. The structure of the League discouraged collective and decisive action against aggressors. Factors outside its control, such as the Great Depression, affected the role of the League. Major crises such as the invasions of Manchuria and Abyssinia and the failure of the World Disarmament Conference finally doomed the League.

The failure of the League can be attributed to a combination of three significant factors. Flaws in the Covenant pertaining to the League's structure limited its power and affected enforcement of its decisions. Furthermore, support for collective security among the major powers was half-hearted. Finally, the League's failure to resolve the Manchurian and Abyssinian crises meant that it was discredited at the very time it was most needed — to halt the rise of Nazism.

Drafting the Body

With a completed Point-form Outline, it is an easy task to draft the body of your essay. On the previous two pages we explained how the outlines provide a flexible formula for creating the paragraph structure for an introduction. Below we have reproduced part of "B. III Failure to resolve crises" from page 36 to illustrate how the outlines shape the paragraphs of the body of a major essay. In the diagram on the next page, notice how the subsections of the Skeleton Outline provide the paragraph structure, while the details of the Point-form Outline supply the supporting evidence for each paragraph. The transformation of B. III from outline to paragraphed copy is shown on the following pages. **Only a single section of the body** is demonstrated because space precludes reproducing the whole essay.

This formula is not a rigid prescription for paragraphing; the detailed outlines simply provide a guide to developing a clear, coherent system. Some organizing scheme is essential because paragraphing remains one of the major difficulties encountered by students. There can never be a fixed and predetermined number of paragraphs in an essay. Every essay is unique and the paragraph structure of each essay will be determined by your research, your thinking, and your shaping of the argument.

B. III Failure to resolve crises

1. Manchuria (powerlessness)
   - Western policy of non-recognition
   - unwilling to use force against Japan
   - Japan leaves League

2. Abyssinia (secret diplomacy)
   - need for Italian support
   - reluctance to impose oil embargo
   - Hoare-Laval plan

3. Loss of public confidence
   - peace ballot shows support
   - disillusionment after Hoare-Laval

B. III Failure to resolve crises	**(introductory paragraph)**
1.Manchuria (powerlessness) - Western policy of non-recognition - unwilling to use force against Japan - Japan leaves League	**(paragraph)**
2. Abyssinia (secret diplomacy) - need for Italian support - reluctance to impose oil embargo - Hoare-Laval plan	**(paragraph)**
3. Loss of public confidence - peace ballot shows support - disillusionment after Hoare-Laval	**(paragraph)**
4. Inequality of member states - lack of racial equality clause - League primarily serving Europe	**(paragraph)**
	(concluding paragraph)

The structural problems of the League of Nations and the duplicity of the major powers became apparent during both the Manchurian and Abyssinian crises. The League's failure to resolve these disputes in a manner consistent with its charter resulted in the loss of both public and political confidence in the organization, discrediting it at the time when it was most needed — the beginning of Hitler's expansion in Europe.

The Japanese invasion of Manchuria in September 1931 and the establishment the following year of the puppet state of Manchukuo presented the League with a conflict between two Pacific powers. One member, Japan, had violated the territorial rights of another, China. But, instead of invoking corrective force, the Western powers who controlled the League and had commercial ties with Japan, merely refused to recognize Manchukuo. In the words of F.P. Walters (1952), "the aggression had taken place, vast territories had been taken from the victim, and yet all they had done was to refuse to recognize the new state" (499). The League was not prepared to take decisive action and provoke a crisis in a region where the commercial interests of its influential members might be at risk. Japan's reaction was to resign from the League, further weakening the international organization.

Mussolini's invasion of Abyssinia in October 1935 was, like Manchuria, a clear case of aggression by one member against another. Britain and France were not prepared to risk their relations with Italy at a time when Nazi Germany increasingly appeared to threaten European security. While they were prepared to condemn Mussolini's aggression against Abyssinia, Britain and France refused to take decisive action and impose an oil embargo. Worse still, Britain and France, in secret negotiations outside the forum of the League, were attempting to placate Italy. When the Hoare-Laval Plan which granted parts of Abyssinia to Italy was exposed, it also revealed the duplicitous nature of Franco-British policy. The Abyssinian crisis was a decisive event in the decline of the League.

The League of Nations enjoyed widespread support as a mechanism for resolving the Abyssinian crisis. In Britain, a "peace ballot" had been held, indicating vast popular support for the League. The Hoare-Laval plan was viewed by the public as government betrayal and as a sign of incompatibility between the spirit of the League and the reality of European diplomacy. Disillusionment set in and British public support for the League was "cast adrift as the government attempted to cover the tracks of its duplicity and confusion, following the path of appeasement and gradual rearmament" (Egerton, 1983, 514).

The European treatment of both Manchuria and Abyssinia demonstrated the inequality of member states in the League. Inequality was actually built into the organization because the architects of the League refused to enshrine racial equality in the Covenant. The violation of the territorial integrity of any member state deserved condemnation and appropriate action. Before taking such action, however, European powers first appeared to assess the diplomatic, political, and commercial costs. The nations of Europe, especially those with colonial interests, seemed far better served by the League of Nations than those states on the periphery of power.

The failure of the League to resolve the conflicts in Manchuria and Abyssinia in a manner consistent with both the spirit and the content of the Covenant discredited the organization. The failure of collective security, coinciding with the expansion of Hitler's Germany, finally doomed the League. It was sadly ironic that in the latter part of the decade many European nations would suffer the same fate as Manchuria and Abyssinia.

You will notice from the previous example that each major section of the body follows a miniature ABC structure. An introductory paragraph introduces the section, "body" paragraphs develop the main point ("the League's failure to solve major crises"), and a concluding paragraph sums up the section. The ABC formula also operates at the individual paragraph level. A topic sentence clearly states the main idea, followed by sentences that provide supporting detail. A concluding sentence sums up the paragraph and clarifies its role in the development of your thesis and may also act as a transition to the next paragraph.

Paragraphs are like links in a chain. Just as a chain is only as strong as its weakest link, so is your essay only as effective as its weakest paragraph. Give unity and cohesion to your paragraphs by eliminating what is irrelevant to the main idea or focal point of each paragraph. Subheadings tend to fragment the unity of an essay. With proper paragraphing, there is no need for subheadings in an essay and instructors usually discourage them. Paragraphs with a central focus, explicit topic sentences, and suitable transitional words provide the unity, flow, and signposts that prevent the reader from getting lost in a maze of words. The clarity of your argument is largely a function of the structure of your material and the style of its presentation. Paragraphs provide the bridging between style and structure, and significantly enhance clarity.

The body of the essay is the most important section and the longest. It is devoted entirely to the development and substantiation of the thesis that was stated at the end of the introduction — that is **the sole function of the body of the essay**. Successful essays have the focus and clarity of a laser beam, not the chaotic brilliance of a fireworks display. Give your essay that focus and clarity by explicitly linking all the ideas and information to your thesis and anchoring your argument in relevant evidence and examples. Instructors look for incisive analysis and argument in an essay, not for chronological narrative, rambling descriptions, or irrelevant biographical details.

Remember that your chief responsibility is to construct and advance a systematic, logical, and convincing thesis — one that is carefully structured, convincingly argued, substantiated with evidence, and clearly expressed.

Drafting the Conclusion

In the final section you weave together the various threads of the thesis and sum up the major supporting points. It should not be a dull summary of the major sections but a subtle linking of the major conclusions that you developed in the body. Sometimes it can be effective to restate the research question since this reminds the reader of the purpose of the essay. But try to be more original than starting with a worn phrase such as, "in conclusion."

Do not add new information in the conclusion to support your thesis since this will confuse the reader. If the information is important, it should be included in the development of the thesis in the body, and not added as an afterthought to the conclusion. Also ensure that any quotations have a specific function, and that they are not simply inserted in the conclusion for dramatic effect. In addition to summing up the thesis, you might place your issue within a wider context or show the broader significance of your work. You could also identify unresolved questions or suggest new questions or indicate interesting aspects for further investigation.

The conclusion is brief, usually one paragraph, but it is important because it is the last opportunity to impress the reader with the validity of your arguments. Remember that last impressions are usually lasting impressions. Below you will find the conclusion of the League of Nations essay.

The League of Nations was a bold attempt to provide a mechanism for maintaining collective security following the devastation of the First World War. Unfortunately, the League was unable to fulfill its mandate due to the combination of serious flaws in the Covenant that severely limited the exercise of its authority and by the determination of a number of member states to pursue an independent diplomatic agenda. Global society requires a means of curbing the competing interests of major powers and protecting the needs of weaker states. The League, despite its failures, was a noble experiment and an important step towards the realization of a more secure international society.

Title Page

Reflect carefully on the phrasing of the title and ensure that it clearly indicates to the reader the focus of your essay. Keep the title precise and concise, and use a subtitle only if it helps clarify the title. Normally the title is not phrased in question form. The title page should be simple and neat. Avoid the use of pictures and photographs. The following information is usually required on title pages:

- Title
- Name
- Course/Class
- Teacher/Instructor
- School/College/University
- Date

**The League of Nations and Collective Security:
Failure of a Dream**

S.M. Conway
History 101

Professor Z. Arbenz
Norwood College
April 2001

Table of Contents

A contents page provides the reader with an outline of the structure of your essay and lists supplementary features, such as the list of sources and the appendix. The contents page follows the title page and abstract (if used). The letters of the alphabet in our example below correspond to the organization used throughout the research and outlining stages. Avoid using the term "Body" in your table of contents. It was used in the research and in the outlines to assist you in understanding the structure of an essay. Short essays seldom require a table of contents and some instructors do not even insist on a contents page for longer papers. Consult your instructor about requirements for the table of contents. There is usually no need to include page references, unless you are writing a major paper or a dissertation.

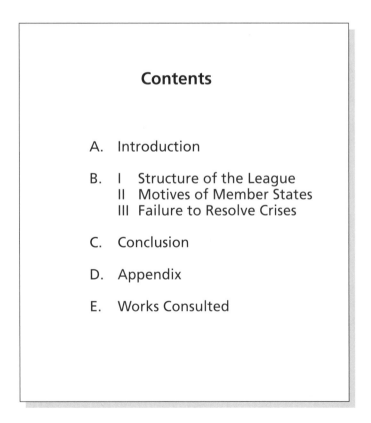

Contents

A. Introduction

B. I   Structure of the League
    II   Motives of Member States
    III Failure to Resolve Crises

C. Conclusion

D. Appendix

E. Works Consulted

Illustrations

Illustrations can be effective in essays. There are two major types of illustrations: tables and figures. **Tables** contain columns of statistical data. **Figures** consist of photographs, maps, drawings, graphs, diagrams, charts, and pictures. Examples of various types of illustrations are shown on pages 123–128 in the appendix.

Tables and figures are usually inserted at the appropriate place in the text of the essay. If they are lengthy, they can be placed in the appendix. Select illustrations carefully and do not overwhelm your essay with too many pictures, statistics, and graphs. Ask yourself whether each table or figure actually illustrates a point in your essay. Consult your instructor about the use and positioning of illustrations if you are in doubt.

Appendix

The appendix is a useful place at the end of your essay for important information that is too extensive to be placed in the body. The material must be relevant to the thesis of your paper and must be cross-referenced in either a footnote or a parenthetical reference. Guard against the temptation to pack the appendix with unnecessary material.

A history paper might include a speech or a chronology of events in the appendix. Statistical tables might be placed in the appendices of geography and economics essays. The appendix is placed before the endnotes (if used) and the bibliography, and each section is numbered and titled. See pages 107–151 of this manual for an example.

❖ ❖ ❖

Ensure that you have incorporated **all the sections and features** of your essay in the rough draft. Revising, editing and preparing the final copy will be much quicker and easier if you have roughed out the **complete essay.** Check carefully to ensure that the rough draft conforms to all the criteria against which the essay will be assessed.

Revising and Editing

Once you have completed your rough draft, you are ready to start revising and editing. The clarity of the argument you are developing and presenting is determined largely by the structure of your answer and the style of your expression. Revising involves reviewing the draft for **structure and organization**. Editing involves refining the **style and expression** of the revised draft. These are important stages for preparing a quality essay, and you must allow time in your schedule for revising and editing.

Set the draft aside for a few days before starting to revise it. Getting a little "distance" allows you to reflect on the draft and will sharpen your eye considerably. If you based your rough draft on a Point-form Outline, you will reduce the amount of revising substantially. The extra work that went into the preparation invariably pays off in the long run.

Your first task is to examine the order of the main sections of the body. Although you may have rearranged the sections of the Point-form Outline, the order might still appear disjointed in the rough draft. The question to ask yourself is whether there is a smooth, logical flow in the sequence of the sections. Check the introduction to make sure that the problem, the purpose and your point of view are clearly spelled out. Does the conclusion sum up the main points of the argument and provide an effective culmination to the essay?

Once you are satisfied with the overall structure, look closely at the paragraphing. Circle the topic sentence in each paragraph to ensure that there is a central focal point. Is there sufficient supporting detail in each paragraph? Is there unity to each paragraph? Are all topic sentences linked to the thesis? Is there a natural flow in the sequence of the paragraphs? Is there any repetitious or contradictory information? Are there any vague and general observations? Do the quotations fit? Are the illustrations relevant? These are the types of questions you should ask yourself as you revise the rough draft. But above all, ask yourself whether the essay **develops and delivers a clear and convincing point of view.**

If you have made many changes, it may be necessary to rewrite a handwritten draft. Revising a word-processed draft is much easier. Revising and rewriting drafts is not wasted time, because **the quality of the essay will improve with each draft.** Prominent writers repeatedly emphasize the importance of revising and editing. William Zinsser points out that "rewriting is the essence of writing well"[8] and Strunk and White stress that "revising is part of writing."[9]

Since editing is largely concerned with fine-tuning and polishing your language and expression, you should read the section on Style on pages 101–104. It is a good practice to have a thesaurus, a dictionary, a manual of style, and a guide to discriminatory language at hand when you are editing your draft. Read through your revised draft slowly, concentrating carefully on the text as you edit.

- Are the spelling and grammar correct?
- Does the punctuation improve the flow of the essay?
- Have you chosen your words carefully?
- Have you eliminated unnecessary words and phrases?
- Is your draft free of discriminatory language?
- Can you vary the structure and length of sentences?
- Is capitalization consistent?
- Can you substitute active for passive verbs?
- Are the verb tenses consistent?
- Have you eliminated contractions?

The next step is to read your draft aloud. You can read it to yourself or tape record it. You may read it to someone else or perhaps have that person read it while you listen. If it is difficult to read and sounds stilted, edit the draft until it **flows smoothly and naturally.** Ask a friend to review the draft, because an independent critic will often detect flaws that pass unnoticed by the writer. Once the editing is complete, read the essay aloud another time. An essay that "speaks well" is invariably an essay that reads well. By eliminating "static" and giving your essay rhythm and resonance, you can dramatically enhance the impact of the message.[10]

The word processor is an invaluable writing tool. It can speed up the revising and editing process, and enhance the quality of your assignments. The advantage of word processing is that once the information is typed, revision and editing can be done without rewriting and retyping the draft. But it is essential to do the preliminary structuring, outlining, and drafting. A word processor has more important uses than simply cutting and pasting paragraphs in a disorganized piece of writing.

It is not always easy to get a feel for the overall structure of an essay on a computer monitor, nor is it easy to detect punctuation or spelling errors. You should revise and edit on a printed copy of the draft as well as on the screen. Using the draft function, you can triple-space your copy and also create wider margins to make space for corrections and comments. Another advantage of a printed copy is that it is easier to read aloud. It can also be read and checked by others. You can then make the changes on the screen and print another copy for further editing.

If you are revising and editing on a computer, you may wish to keep all your electronic drafts. In this case simply name each revision, such as "LofN1," and "LofN2," and so on. This will allow you to return to earlier versions for material that you deleted in later revisions. After you have produced your final copy, you can erase the earlier files. Alternatively, you could keep printed copies of earlier versions.

Whether you are printing copies or editing on the screen, it is important that you frequently **save your draft** on both the hard drive and on a floppy disk to avoid losing your essay if there is a power failure or your hard drive malfunctions. Instructors no longer accept the excuse of a "computer crash." Also unacceptable is the excuse that the essay could not be printed because the printer ran out of ink or paper.

If your word processor has a spell check, a thesaurus or a grammar check program, take advantage of it when you are editing. It will often find errors and provide useful suggestions, but it cannot provide a guarantee for the quality of your essay. Some software may not be able to detect the difference between "to," "too," and "two" or between "cite," "sight," and "site." It remains your responsibility to edit your work carefully, regardless of the software you use.

The Final Copy

Leave yourself enough time to set aside your edited draft for a few days before you prepare the final copy. Producing the final copy is simply finalizing the edited draft — it is the final tuning of the essay. If you have followed a systematic process of researching, outlining, drafting, revising, and editing, preparing the final copy should be quick and pain-less, especially if you use a word processor. Converting the rough draft to the final copy is the real test of the advice repeated throughout this manual: **the more time and effort you expend initially, the less is needed at the end.**

Your completed essay is the product of a lengthy process. Much of the process never appears in the final copy, but the process is nevertheless essential to the quality of the essay.[*] Although the process — in the form of notes, outlines, and drafts — is sometimes evaluated, frequently instructors will base their assessment solely on the essay that is submitted — the one tenth of the iceberg above the water. If one tenth counts for 100 percent, then it is especially important that you package the final copy with painstaking care.

Computer technology will enhance the appearance of your essay. Software programs facilitate attractive layout of text and illustrations, and modern printers support a variety of font styles and ensure a clean, professional type. Most schools and universities have computer facilities that are accessible to students, so there is no need to purchase expensive equipment. Combining literary ability with typing and computing skills is an important asset today. Remember, however, that it is **substance that characterizes a good essay.** Technological dazzle alone is insufficient.

Individual instructors sometimes have their own preferences with regard to format, so check manuscript requirements again before starting the final copy. If your instructor has expressed no specific preference, consider formatting your essay as outlined on the next page.

---

[*] Keep your notes, outlines, and drafts: they are your best defence against a charge of plagiarism. Always keep a backup copy of your essay as well.

- Use standard-sized white unlined paper.

- Type double-space on one side of the page only.

- Use a common font like Times New Roman and a standard font size, usually 12 point.

- Leave at least a 2.5 cm or 1-inch margin all the way around the page.

- Number pages accurately in the top right-hand corner.

- Avoid section headings, as they tend to disrupt the argument.

- If headings are used, ensure that they are consistent in style and size.

- Do not leave white spaces between the introduction and the body and between the body and the conclusion. Your paragraphs should act as signposts to the reader.

- Left justify your text, leaving a "ragged" right margin. This is easier to read than full justified margins, which can create uneven spacing.

- Use a paperclip to hold your pages together if you are using endnotes, because some instructors like to remove the endnotes and refer to them as they read the essay.

- Use a single staple in the top left corner to hold your pages together if you are not using endnotes.

- If in doubt about manuscript requirements, consult your instructor.

Proofread your essay meticulously from title page to bibliography. You might ask a friend to do a second proofreading. Frequent errors create a poor impression and will have a negative effect on the evaluation of the essay. On the other hand, an error-free and attractively laid-out essay will make a positive impact on the reader. The extra time devoted to revising, editing, and proofreading your essay is well worth it. There is a close relationship between effort and quality, and a good piece of work will always reflect the time and care taken in its preparation.

QUOTATIONS

Researchers rely on both original (or primary) sources and on previous scholarship in the form of secondary sources when exploring issues in the humanities and the social sciences. An important decision facing students is when to use paraphrased ideas and information and when to quote directly from the source material. Quotations, from either primary or secondary sources, can be effectively used in the following situations:

- As evidence to illustrate and provide credibility for your arguments.
- To add authority to your point of view.
- To lend elegance and eloquence to your writing.
- To quote the author's central argument when challenging an opposing viewpoint.
- Where the original words better express the meaning than is possible by paraphrasing.

A cardinal rule in writing essays and papers is: **Do not overquote.** Parachuting quotations into the essay simply as space-fillers or for dramatic effect will destroy its clarity. Also avoid name-dropping of authorities for effect. Comments from authorities may indicate the breadth and depth of your research but "to indulge yourself too often in the quoting of others' great thoughts is to run the risk of never learning to formulate your own."[11] It is your interpretations and ideas that the instructor wants to read.

Quotations alone do not constitute indisputable evidence, nor do they speak for themselves. Therefore, quotations must be firmly anchored in the text of your essay and explicitly linked to the thesis. Do not just dangle quotations in front of your reader; introduce each quotation by identifying the work or author, place it in context, and explain it. It is the strength of **your** arguments that will finally convince the reader of the validity of your thesis. Does each quotation serve a purpose? If not, eliminate it.

Not only should you select your quotations carefully, but you should keep them short. If you decide to quote a primary excerpt or a secondary expert, select only the essential words and use ellipses (. . .) as shown in the Alderson example opposite. Remember that clarity of argument is your key objective. Cluttering your essay with lengthy quotations — no matter how relevant — does not promote clarity.

Integrating your quotations smoothly into the text of the essay can enhance clarity. Short quotations of less than forty words or less than four lines should be merged as naturally as possible into the text of the essay and enclosed within quotation marks, as shown below.

Economist Janine Velasquez argues that "floating exchange rates facilitate global trade."

Longer quotations of more than forty words or four lines should be separated from the text as shown in the example on the next page. The quoted passage (also known as a block quotation) starts on a new line and is usually introduced with a colon. Quotation marks are omitted. A block quotation is indented between four and ten spaces from the left margin, depending on the preferences of your instructor or on the recommendation of the manual you are using. The Modern Language Association (MLA) recommends a ten-space indention, *A Manual for Writers* by Kate Turabian suggests four spaces, while The American Psychological Association (APA) requires a five-space indention. For simplicity, it may be easier to use either one or two tab stops for indenting block quotations.

Once again, there is no consensus on spacing block quotations. MLA recommends double-spacing, *A Manual for Writers* suggests single-spacing, while APA accepts either single or double-spacing. Check spacing requirements with your instructor if you are uncertain. Illustrated below is an example of a block quotation.

Alderson, who commanded the regiment for most of its tour of duty, wrote to Lessard:

> **I have just come back from the station where I went to see your people off . . . and I should like to write and tell you how very sincerely sorry I am that they have left. We have soldiered together for seven months . . . and during that time a firm bond developed.**

If it is necessary to omit part of a quotation because of length or irrelevance, use three spaced periods (. . .) as shown in the previous example. This is known as an **ellipsis.** However, you must not alter the meaning of the passage or make it incomprehensible through your own omission of words. You must also ensure that the modified quotation is grammatically correct.

It is sometimes necessary to insert a word or phrase in a quotation for clarification or correction. If you have to insert words in a quotation to clarify its meaning, enclose them in square brackets.

"The role [of the Mounted Infantry] is to act as an advance guard."

If an error is present in the quoted material, use the Latin word *"sic"* (meaning "so" or "thus") to indicate the error. If *"sic"* is placed within the quotation, enclose it in square brackets and if *"sic"* falls outside the quotation, then enclose it in parentheses, as demonstrated below. Either italicize or underline *"sic."*

"The Police Chief denied that the prisonners [sic] had been refused water."

Clark contends that "The Charter of Rights has compromised the notion of parliamentary sovereinty" (sic).

Single quotation marks are used where a quotation occurs within quoted material, as shown below. In a block quotation, where opening and closing quotation marks are omitted, any additional quoted material is enclosed in double quotation marks.

"Noble wrote in his diary that he had been subjected to 'cruel and unusual punishment' during his confinement."

Generally, punctuation marks such as commas and periods are placed within the quotation marks, while colons, semicolons, question marks, and exclamation marks go outside the quotation marks. However, any punctuation mark that is part of the quoted material is included within the quotation marks.

Do not burden the text with excessively long quotations over seven or ten lines long; they should be placed in the appendix and referred to in a note or a parenthetical reference. Always ask yourself whether a long quotation is essential or whether you could shorten it by the use of ellipses, or even eliminate it.

There are several ways you can distance yourself from quotations or ideas that are discriminatory. You can paraphrase the remark, replace the discriminatory words with bracketed substitutes, or use only the non-offensive words. If you need to quote in full, then use *"(sic)"* to indicate the inappropriate words.[12]

It is essential that you quote the material, including punctuation, **accurately.** To alter the wording or meaning of a quotation or to use a quotation out of context is unethical. Therefore, it is important that you transcribe quotations carefully during the analysis and recording. To use the writing and ideas of other authors without acknowledgment is not only unethical, but illegal. There are procedures for acknowledging your sources so that you avoid charges of plagiarism. These citation procedures have been omitted from the quotation examples above to avoid confusion. They are explained in detail in the next section on Documentation.

The most common conventions for quoting have been covered in this section. For more complex forms, students should consult the *MLA Handbook*, A *Manual for Writers*, the APA *Publication Manual*, or the instructor. Above all, be consistent in the method you use for quoting. Finally, remember **to use quotations sparingly and judiciously.** Consider whether paraphrasing or summarizing a point might be more effective than quoting it. A paper comprising numerous quotations woven together like a patchwork quilt is not an essay.

Documentation

Introduction

The sources of the information and the ideas that you use to develop and substantiate your arguments must be identified and acknowledged. Not only must direct quotations be documented, paraphrased ideas and important factual details that you may have borrowed from other writers and researchers must also be documented. It is especially important to document the source of your evidence when you are developing a controversial point.

Plagiarism is the unacknowledged use of someone else's ideas: it is a serious academic offence. Just as ignorance of the law is no excuse, there is no excuse for "accidental" plagiarism. Careful documentation will help you avoid charges of plagiarism. Since each of your notes was coded with a source and page reference, it is easy to acknowledge all important details and ideas in your essay.

Factual information that is common knowledge need not be documented. For instance, you do not have to document a source stating that the League of Nations was founded in 1919. Frequently, determining what is common knowledge is not easy, but your judgment will improve with experience and practice. "Document when in doubt" is a safe route to follow, but do not overdo the use of citations. It is a mistake to attempt to impress the reader with reams of footnotes or parenthetical citations. Likewise, a lengthy list of sources in the bibliography, instead of inspiring awe, may arouse suspicion. Be guided by common sense as well as ethics when documenting your sources.[13]

Two key elements are used in documentation: the **citation** and the **list of sources.**

- The **citation** is a brief reference in the text of the essay identifying the source of the information, idea or quotation. Either a parenthetical (bracketed) reference or a number is used.

- The **list of sources** is placed at the end of the essay and provides details of the in-text citations and may include other sources used to prepare the assignment.

Two major documentation or citation systems (or styles) are used in the humanities and the social sciences: the **numbered footnote/endnote** system and the **parenthetical author-date** system.*

- **Footnotes/Endnotes:** The source is indicated by using a superscript number in the text, which corresponds to an entry in a footnote or an endnote containing complete bibliographic details. These details are repeated in a slightly different order in an alphabetical list of sources (or bibliography) at the end of the essay.

- **Author-Date:** The source is indicated by providing the author's last name and the year of publication of the work in a parenthetical citation in the text of the essay. A page reference is also included. The reader can then refer to an alphabetical list of sources (or references) at the end of the essay to obtain complete bibliographic details. This method, popularized by the American Psychological Association (APA), is widely known as "APA style."

Students often find the documentation of sources a baffling process. To illustrate the differences in **citing sources** in the author-date style and the numbered footnote style, we have reproduced identical paragraphs from the League of Nations sample essay (pages 47–48) opposite. Examples of endnotes can be found on page 152. To see how the **sources are listed** at the end of an essay in the numbered note and author-date systems, refer to pages 86 and 99.

---

* There are two other major documentation styles. The parenthetical Author-Page system, developed by the Modern Language Association (MLA), is widely used in language and literature. The numbered Citation-Sequence system is used mainly in the natural and physical sciences.

... In the words of F.P. Walters (1952)," the aggression had taken place, vast territories had been taken from the victim, and yet all they had done was to refuse to recognize the new state" (499). The League was not prepared to take decisive action and provoke a crisis in a region where the commercial interests of its influential members might be at risk. Japan's reaction was to resign from the League, further weakening the organization.

The League enjoyed widespread support as a mechanism for resolving the Abyssinian crisis. In Britain, a "peace ballot" had been held, indicating vast popular support for the League. The Hoare-Laval plan was viewed by the public as government betrayal and as a sign of incompatibility between the spirit of the League and the reality of European diplomacy. Disillusionment set in and British public support for the League was "cast adrift as the government attempted to cover the tracks of its duplicity and confusion, following the path of appeasement and gradual rearmament" (Egerton, 1983, 514).

... In the words of F.P. Walters," the aggression had taken place, vast territories had been taken from the victim, and yet all they had done was to refuse to recognize the new state."[8] The League was not prepared to take decisive action and provoke a crisis in a region where the commercial interests of its influential members might be at risk. Japan's reaction was to resign from the League, further weakening the organization.

The League of Nations enjoyed widespread support as a mechanism for resolving the Abyssinian crisis. In Britain, a "peace ballot" had been held, indicating vast popular support for the League. The Hoare-Laval plan was viewed by the public as government betrayal and as a sign of incompatibility between the spirit of the League and the reality of European diplomacy. Disillusionment set in and British public support for the League was "cast adrift as the government attempted to cover the tracks of its duplicity and confusion, following the path of appeasement and gradual rearmament."[9]

---

[8]F.P. Walters, A History of the League of Nations (Oxford: Oxford UP, 1952), 499.

[9]George W. Egerton, "Collective Security as Political Myth: Liberal Internationalism and The League of Nations in Politics and History," International History Review 5 (1983):514.

Documenting your sources can serve a number of functions:

- The information can be checked for accuracy.
- Other writers get credit for their ideas.
- Basing your research on sound scholarship will enhance its credibility.
- Readers are guided to additional sources of information on the topic.

Electronic resources are expanding at a remarkable rate. These sources can be divided into two main groups:

- **Portable databases,** such as CD-ROMs, which may be shared via a network.
- **Online material** available on the Internet and accessible by a computer, a modem and a browser through a service provider. Online information is also available, usually for a fee, from a service such as *Dialog,* either by dial-up access or through the Internet.

Like traditional sources used in an essay, electronic sources must be documented. Documenting portable databases, such as CD-ROMs, is not that different from documenting other types of sources. However, documentation procedures for online sources are considerably more complex, and separate sections (pages 80–85 and 96–98) have been devoted to these procedures. The nature and evaluation of electronic sources is covered under "Sources" (pages 116–117) in the Appendix.

The **numbered footnote/endnote** system and the **parenthetical author-date** system (or "APA style") are described separately in the pages ahead. Each system is structured similarly under the following headings:

1. Citing sources   2. Listing sources
3. Online sources   4. Explanatory notes

Refer to pages 67–87 for an explanation of the footnote/endnote system, and see pages 88–100 for the author-date system.   Always check with your instructor to determine the preferred method of documentation for each essay. Remember, whichever method you choose, to follow the method consistently throughout your essay. And finally, strive for accuracy, simplicity, and clarity when documenting your sources.

Footnotes/Endnotes

Citing Sources

Sources can be acknowledged by a numbered note system. A number is placed above the line at the end of the sentence or quotation, and these citation references are numbered consecutively throughout the paper. The superscript numbers follow all punctuation marks except the dash. Each of these numbers corresponds to an entry, either in a footnote at the bottom of the page or in an endnote near the end of the essay. Numbered documentary or citation notes create less interruption in the reader's flow of thought than the parenthetical author-date procedure.

Traditionally, footnotes, rather than endnotes, have been used to cite information and ideas. Information in a footnote is more accessible than in an endnote, and this is especially true when reading dissertations in microform. Word processing programs make it relatively easy to use the footnote format. See the examples at the bottom of page 65.

Footnotes are placed at the bottom of the page and separated from the text by a solid line approximately twenty spaces in length. Leave a blank line and indent the footnote the same number of spaces as your regular paragraph indentions or use a single tab space. Two methods may be followed in numbering footnotes, as illustrated below. In the first example, the number is typed on the line, followed by a period and a space, and then the author and publication details are entered. The traditional style is to use a superscript number without a period or a space as shown in the second example.

Example:

1. Sylvia Ostry, *The Post-Cold War Trading System: Who's on First?* (Chicago: University of Chicago Press, 1997), 59.

[1]Sylvia Ostry, *The Post-Cold War Trading System: Who's on First?* (Chicago: University of Chicago Press, 1997), 59.

Notes that continue on a second line start at the left margin and are single-spaced, but you should leave a double space between individual footnotes. Use a slightly smaller font size for your footnotes than the regular type used in the essay.

Another method is to use **endnotes** and place all citations on a separate page just before the final list of sources. Title the page "Notes" and enter the details as explained above for footnotes. Superscript numbers are not normally used in endnotes. Type the number on the line followed by a period and a space, and then enter the citation details. See page 152 of this manual for an example of endnotes. If you are using the numbered note system to cite your sources, check with your instructor whether the citations should be placed in footnotes or in endnotes.

How many citations should there be in an essay is a common question. There is no magic number of citations in an essay. The number will be determined by the nature of the evidence — whether it is controversial or common knowledge, whether the ideas are original or not, or by the number of direct quotations. The lack of rigid rules for citing may be initially disconcerting for you, but your judgment will improve with practice and experience.

When a work is mentioned in a note for the first time, provide the complete citation. Subsequent references to a source use a shortened form, as explained on page 73. If there is no place of publication given, use "n.p." and for no publisher also use "n.p." If both are missing, it is permissible to use just "n.p." If no date is provided for the source, insert "n.d."

Samples of the more common forms of citation (or documentary or reference) notes are provided on the following pages. These examples are based largely on the procedures described in *A Manual for Writers* by Kate Turabian and in *The Chicago Manual of Style*. The *MLA Handbook* also contains a section on numbered citation notes. Increasingly, abbreviations are being used to simplify documentation procedures. For example, it is acceptable to shorten "Oxford University Press" to "Oxford UP" according to MLA. We have used both the short and the full forms in our examples.

BOOK

ONE AUTHOR

[1]Alastair Iain Johnston, *Cultural Realism: Strategic Culture and Grand Strategy in Chinese History* (Princeton: Princeton UP, 1995), 64.

TWO AUTHORS

[2]James Blight and David Welch, *On the Brink: Americans and Soviets Reexamine the Cuban Missile Crisis* (New York: Hill & Wang, 1989), 23.

MORE THAN THREE AUTHORS/EDITORS

[3]Joshua Brown et al., *History from South Africa: Alternative Visions and Practices* (Philadelphia: Temple University Press, 1991), 38.

EDITOR/COMPILER/TRANSLATOR

[4]Anne Krueger, ed., *The WTO as an International Organization* (Chicago: U of Chicago P, 1998), 32.

NO AUTHOR

[5]*Beowulf*, trans. David Wright (Harmondsworth, U.K: Penguin, 1960), 45. (Do not use "Anonymous" or "Anon.")

CORPORATE AUTHOR

[6]American Psychological Association, *Publication Manual*, 4th ed. (Washington, DC: American Psychological Association, 1994), 8.

MULTIVOLUME WORK

[7]Will and Ariel Durant, *The Story of Civilization,* vol. 10, *Rousseau and Revolution* (New York: Simon and Schuster, 1965), 56.

ESSAY IN AN EDITED WORK

[8]Christopher Wrigley, "Changes in East African Society," in *A History of East Africa*, ed. D.A. Low and Alison Smith (Oxford: Oxford University Press, 1976), 508.

LATER EDITION

[9]Mary-Claire van Leunen, *A Handbook for Scholars*, rev. ed. (New York: Oxford University Press, 1992), 49.

PAMPHLET/MONOGRAPH

[10]Danielle Lacasse and Antonio Lechasseur, *The National Archives of Canada, 1872–1997*, Historical Booklet, no. 58 (Ottawa: Canadian Historical Association, 1997), 5.

OTHER LANGUAGE

[11]Heinz Kosok, *Geschichte der anglo-irischen Literatur* (Berlin: Erich Schmidt, 1960), 51.

ENCYCLOPEDIA

[12]Manfred Jones, "Isolationism," *Encyclopedia of American Foreign Policy*, 1978 ed.

YEARBOOK

[13]Michael D. Yapko, "Repressed Memories: Special Report," *Britannica Book of the Year 1995* (Chicago: Encyclopaedia Britannica, 1996), 201.

NEWSPAPER

ARTICLE

[14]Duncan Baxter, "Generation Soundbite," *Times* (London), 1 January 1999, 28.

EDITORIAL

[15]"Discordant Accord," editorial, *Times of India*, 28 December 1998, 9.

LETTER TO THE EDITOR

[16]B.Traister, letter, *Globe and Mail* (Toronto), 16 January 1999, D6.

MAGAZINE

SIGNED ARTICLE

[18]Gideon Rahman, "Indonesia: A Survey," *The Economist*, 17 April 1993, 9.

UNSIGNED ARTICLE

[19]"Quark Hunters," *Time*, 29 October 1990, 36.

JOURNAL

CONTINUOUS PAGINATION

[20]I.L. Claude, "Casual Commitment to International Relations," *Political Science Quarterly* 96 (1981): 370.

SEPARATE PAGINATION

[21]Martin Feldstein, "Refocusing the IMF," *Foreign Affairs* 77, no. 2 (1998): 23.

NEWSLETTER

[22]John Reid, "Historians and the National Archives of Canada," *Bulletin of the Canadian Historical Association* 16, no. 4 (1990): 7.

REVIEW

BOOK

[23]Anthony Appiah, review of *Africa: A Biography of the Continent*, by John Reader, *New York Review of Books*, XLV, no. 20 (17 December 1998): 66.

FILM

[24]David Ansen, "How the West was Lost," review of *Dances with Wolves* (TIG/Orion movie), *Newsweek*, 19 November 1990, 67.

INTERVIEW

PERSONAL

[25]Edwin McCormick, interview by author, tape recording, Toronto, Ontario, 10 January 1980.

PUBLISHED

[26]Nadine Gordimer, "The Power of a Well-Told Tale," interview by P. Gray and B. Nelan, *Time*, 14 October 1991, 92.

RADIO/TELEVISION

[27]Nadine Gordimer, interview by Eleanor Wachtel, *Writers and Company*, CBC Stereo, 26 May 1991.

CONFERENCE PAPER (UNPUBLISHED)

[28]Jim Fodrea, "Pacific North West Salmon Reservoir Operation Issues," (paper presented at the 1998 International Water Resources Engineering Conference, Reston, VA.)

DISSERTATION

UNPUBLISHED

[29]Justin L. Robertson, "Strategic Industrial Sectors in the World Trading System: The Case of Indonesia" (master's thesis, Dalhousie University, 1998), 27.

ABSTRACT

[30]Keith L. Shimko, "Images and Policy Debates" (Ph. D. diss. Indiana University, 1990), abstract in *Dissertation Abstracts International* 51A (1990): 1766 A.

SPEECH/LECTURE

[31]M. Scott Peck, "A New Psychology of Love, Traditional Values, and Spiritual Growth," Lecture, The Centre of New Fire, Ottawa, 22 September 1990.

FILM

[32]*Dances with Wolves*, dir. Kevin Costner, TIG/Orion, Los Angeles, 1990.

VIDEOCASSETTE

[33]*The Civil War*, dir. Ken Burns, PBS, 1994, videocassette.

RADIO/TELEVISION PROGRAM

[34]"The Human Zoo," *The Human Animal*, narr. Desmond Morris, The Learning Channel, 15 January 1999.

WORK OF ART

[35]Pablo Picasso, *Still Life with Chair-Caning*, oil on canvas, 1912, Musée Picasso, Paris.

SOUND RECORDING

[36]William Shakespeare, *Twelfth Night*, dir. Howard Sackler, Caedmon, SRS-M213, 1961, cassette.

MAP

[37]*Physical United States*, map (Washington, DC: National Geographic Society, 1997).

PUBLIC DOCUMENT

[38]U.S. Library of Congress, *Annual Report of the Librarian of Congress, 1997* (Washington, DC: Government Printing Office, 1997), 59–60.

MANUSCRIPT

[39]Hare to father, 16 April 1900, letter, W.A. Hare Papers, National Archives, Ottawa.

CD-ROM

[40]*Discover the Great Lakes: The Ecosystem of the Great Lakes-St. Lawrence*, CD-ROM (Ottawa: Environment Canada, 1997), Sustainability in Lake Ontario.

INDIRECT SOURCE

[41]L. Curtis, *With Milner in South Africa* (Oxford: Oxford University Press, 1951), 87; quoted in Thomas Pakenham, *The Boer War* (London: Weidenfeld and Nicholson, 1979), 101.

All titles have been italicized in these examples. If you are using a word processor, titles should be italicized. Underline titles in typed essays.

Complete citation details are given in the first reference to a source. However, there is no need to repeat all the details in a subsequent reference. If, for example, you refer to a work by Turabian that you have already cited in full, use an abbreviated format containing the author's surname and the page reference, as shown below.

5. Kate Turabian, *A Manual for Writers of Term Papers, Theses, and Dissertations*, 6th ed. (Chicago: University of Chicago Press, 1996), 99.

6. Turabian, 108.

If more than one of Turabian's books has already been cited, you would have to include a shortened version of the title to identify the specific source.

6. Turabian, *Manual for Writers*, 108.

If it is necessary to refer immediately **to the same source**, you may choose to use "ibid.," which is the abbreviated form of the Latin word "ibidem" meaning "in the same place." For example, an immediate reference to the same page of Turabian's *Manual For Writers* would be cited:

7. ibid.

If a citation from **a different page in the same book** by Turabian follows **immediately**, it would be entered in this way:

8. ibid., 170.

"Ibid." is not italicized or underlined. It is not essential, however, to use "ibid." Instead, simply repeat the author's name and give the new page number. Some instructors do not like the use of "ibid." Other Latin abbreviations such as "op.cit." and "loc.cit." are becoming obsolete. Once again, if you are in doubt, clarify procedures for repeat citations with your instructor.

Listing Sources

As a general rule, it is recommended that you list **all** the sources that proved **useful** in preparing the essay. Traditionally, this list has been called a "**Bibliography**," and the term is still widely used. However, some instructors object to the use of the term for two reasons. First, "bibliography" literally means a list of books, and sources today range from books to interviews to databases. Second, "bibliography" implies a complete list of sources on a topic, and student sources for an essay are unlikely to represent an exhaustive list. Consider using alternative designations, such as the following: "Works Consulted," "Sources," "Select Bibliography," or "References."

Your sources should be listed in alphabetical order by author's last name on a separate page at the end of the essay. **Do not number your sources.** Use a single list of sources for high school and university essays. For longer research papers and dissertations you may be required to classify your sources into primary and secondary material or published and unpublished information. The classified structure of the Working Bibliography recommended earlier in this guide suggested that sources be grouped under headings such as "Books," "Articles" and "Audio-Visual." This division was to encourage a diversity of sources. The final list of sources should not be classified in this way.

The details in a citation note and a corresponding bibliographic entry are usually identical, except for inserting a page reference in the citation note. There are **slight differences** in the format for **citing** your sources in footnotes or endnotes and **listing** your sources in the bibliography, as shown below.

Footnotes/Endnotes

1. Sylvia Ostry, *The Post-Cold War Trading System: Who's on First?* (Chicago: University of Chicago Press, 1997), 59.

Bibliography

Ostry, Sylvia. *The Post-Cold War Trading System: Who's on First?* Chicago: University of Chicago Press, 1997.

The entry for each source starts at the left margin, with the author's last name listed first. If the entry extends beyond the line, the second and subsequent lines are single-spaced and indented five spaces or a single tab stop. Leave a double space between individual entries. If there is no place of publication given use "N.p." and for no publisher use "n.p." If both are missing, it is permissible to use just "N.p." If no date is provided, insert "n.d."

Some instructors may require **a list of sources containing only the works cited in the essay.** If you used endnotes to cite your sources, it would be superfluous to repeat the same details in a slightly different order on the next page. In this case, your citations under "Notes" would serve as a list of cited sources, although they would not be in alphabetical order. If you placed your citations in footnotes, you should still append a separate list of sources headed "Works Cited" or "References." Whether your final list of sources includes only cited sources or all sources that proved useful, "References" is a convenient designation because it includes both categories.

Occasionally, you may quote an isolated idea from a work that has little relevance to the subject of your essay. You should cite the source in a footnote or endnote, but you do not have to enter it in your "Works Consulted" or "References." You will notice that a number of endnotes in this manual do not appear in the Works Consulted section. **Your final list should consist only of those sources that proved useful in preparing the essay.**

You may be required to make critical comments on the merits of each source. Head your list of sources either "Annotated Bibliography" or "Annotated List of Works Cited," depending on the nature of the list of sources.

Dunham, Aileen. *Political Unrest in Upper Canada, 1815-1836.* Toronto: McLelland and Stewart, 1963.

A detailed study of the underlying political events that led to the rebellion in Upper Canada in 1837. It is most useful for an understanding of the political problems of the period. Although dated, it is certainly not an outdated work.

The examples on the following pages are based largely on the procedures described in *The Chicago Manual of Style* and *A Manual for Writers*.

BOOK

ONE AUTHOR

Johnston, Alastair Iain. *Cultural Realism: Strategic Culture and Grand Strategy in Chinese History*. Princeton: Princeton UP, 1995.

TWO AUTHORS

Blight, James and David Welch. *On the Brink: Americans and Soviets Reexamine the Cuban Missile Crisis*. New York: Hill & Wang, 1989.

MORE THAN THREE AUTHORS/EDITORS

Brown, Joshua et al. *History from South Africa: Alternative Visions and Practices*. Philadelphia: Temple UP, 1991.

EDITOR/COMPILER/TRANSLATOR

Krueger, Anne, ed. *The WTO as an International Organization*. Chicago: U of Chicago P, 1998.

NO AUTHOR

Beowulf. Translated by David Wright. Harmondsworth, U.K: Penguin, 1960. (Do not use "Anonymous" or "Anon.")

CORPORATE AUTHOR

American Psychological Association. *Publication Manual*. 4th ed. Washington, DC: American Psychological Association, 1994.

MULTIVOLUME WORK

Durant, Will and Ariel. *The Story of Civilization*. Vol. 10, *Rousseau and Revolution*. New York: Simon and Schuster, 1965.

ESSAY IN AN EDITED WORK

Wrigley, Christopher. "Changes in East African Society." In *A History of East Africa*, ed.   D.A. Low and Alison Smith. Oxford: Oxford University Press, 1976.

LATER EDITION

van Leunen, Mary-Claire. *A Handbook for Scholars*. Rev. ed. New York: Oxford UP, 1992.

PAMPHLET/MONOGRAPH

Lacasse, Danielle and Antonio Lechasseur. *The National Archives of Canada, 1872–1997*. Historical Booklet, no. 58. Ottawa: Canadian Historical Association, 1997.

OTHER LANGUAGE

Kosok, Heinz. *Geschichte der anglo-irischen Literatur*. Berlin: Erich Schmidt, 1960.

ENCYCLOPEDIA

Jones, Manfred. "Isolationism." *Encyclopedia of American Foreign Policy*. 1978 ed.

YEARBOOK

Yapko, Michael D. "Repressed Memories: Special Report." *Britannica Book of the Year 1995*. Chicago: Encyclopaedia Britannica, 1996.

NEWSPAPER

ARTICLE

Baxter, Duncan. "Generation Soundbite." *Times* (London), 1 January 1999, 28.

EDITORIAL

"Discordant Accord." Editorial. *Times of India*, 28 December 1998, 10.

LETTER TO THE EDITOR

Traister, Bryce. Letter. *Globe and Mail* (Toronto), 16 January 1999, D6.

OBITUARY

Allen, William. Obituary. *Times* (London), 1 January 1999, 19.

MAGAZINE

SIGNED ARTICLE

Rahman, Gideon. "Indonesia: A Survey." *The Economist*, 17 April 1993, 3–18.

UNSIGNED ARTICLE

"Quark Hunters." *Time*, 29 October 1990, 36.

JOURNAL

CONTINUOUS PAGINATION

Claude, I.L. "Casual Commitment to International Relations." *Political Science Quarterly 96* (1981): 367–79.

SEPARATE PAGINATION

Feldstein, Martin. "Refocusing the IMF." *Foreign Affairs* 77, no. 2 (1998): 20–33.

NEWSLETTER

Reid, John. "Historians and the National Archives of Canada." *Bulletin of the Canadian Historical Association* 16, no. 4 (1990): 5–12.

REVIEW

BOOK

Appiah, Anthony.   Review of *Africa: A Biography of the Continent*, by John Reader. *New York Review of Books*, XLV, no. 20 (17 December 1998): 64–72.

FILM

Ansen, David. "How the West was Lost." Review of *Dances with Wolves* i.e. (Orion movie). *Newsweek*, 19 November 1990, 67–68.

INTERVIEW

PERSONAL

McCormick, Edwin. Interview by author. Tape recording. Toronto, Ontario, 10 January 1980.

PUBLISHED

Gordimer, Nadine. "The Power of a Well-Told Tale." Interview by P. Gray and B. Nelan. *Time*, 14 October 1991, 92–93.

RADIO/TELEVISION

Gordimer, Nadine. Interview by Eleanor Wachtel. *Writers and Company*. CBC Stereo, 26 May 1991.

CONFERENCE PAPER (UNPUBLISHED)

Fodrea, Jim. "Pacific North West Salmon Reservoir Operation Issues." Paper presented at the 1998 International Water Resources Engineering Conference, Reston, VA.

DISSERTATION

UNPUBLISHED

Robertson, Justin L. "Strategic Industrial Sectors in the World Trading System: The Case of Indonesia." Master's thesis, Dalhousie University, 1998.

ABSTRACT

Shimko, Keith L. "Images and Policy Debates."   Ph. D. diss., Indiana University, 1990. Abstract in *Dissertation Abstracts International* 51A (1990): 1766 A.

SPEECH/LECTURE

Peck, M. Scott. "A New Psychology of Love, Traditional Values, and Spiritual Growth." Lecture. The Centre of New Fire. Ottawa, 22 September 1990.

FILM

Dances with Wolves. Directed by Kevin Costner. TIG/Orion, Los Angeles, 1990.

VIDEOCASSETTE

The Civil War. Directed by Ken Burns. PBS, 1994. Videocassette.

RADIO/TELEVISION PROGRAM

"The Human Zoo." *The Human Animal*. Narrated by Desmond Morris. The Learning Channel, 15 January 1999.

WORK OF ART

Picasso, Pablo. *Still Life with Chair-Caning*. Oil on canvas. 1912. Musée Picasso, Paris.

SOUND RECORDING

Shakespeare,William. *Twelfth Night*. Directed by Howard Sackler. Caedmon, SRS-M213, 1961. Cassette.

MAP

Physical United States. Map. Washington, DC: National Geographic Society, 1997.

PUBLIC DOCUMENT

U.S. Library of Congress. *Annual Report of the Librarian of Congress, 1997*. Washington, DC: Government Printing Office, 1997.

MANUSCRIPT

Hare, W.A. Papers. National Archives, Ottawa.

CD-ROM

Discover the Great Lakes: The Ecosystem of the Great Lakes-St. Lawrence. CD-ROM. Ottawa: Environment Canada, 1997.

INDIRECT SOURCE

Curtis, L. *With Milner in South Africa*. Oxford: Oxford University Press, 1951, 87. Quoted in Thomas Pakenham, *The Boer War*, 101. London: Weidenfeld and Nicholson, 1979.

All titles have been italicized in these examples. If you are using a word processor, titles should be italicized. Underline titles in typed essays.

When listing two or more sources by the same author, enter the name for the first entry only. For the next entry (and successive entries) type an eight-space line in place of the author's name followed by a period. The entries may be arranged alphabetically by title or chronologically. See the Works Consulted on pages 86 and 153 for examples.

Online Sources

Like print or video sources used in an essay, online material must also be documented. As explained on pages 114–117, there are major differences between traditional sources and online sources. Some of these differences directly influence documentation procedures.

Online sources are ephemeral — they may exist today and disappear tomorrow. Online sources are frequently updated and they can be easily modified by adding or deleting details. Furthermore, the access route and the address or URL may change. Because of their fleeting nature and ease of alteration, it is necessary to provide **two dates when citing online sources** — the date of publication or latest revision and the date that you consulted the source.

Since sources frequently disappear or change drastically, you may wish to print copies of your online sources or alternatively save them to disk as confirmation of their existence, brief as it sometimes is. Consider printing just the first page of lengthy documents as proof of their existence.

In printed sources, such as a book, a page reference in a citation note indicates the specific location of important material used in the essay. But page numbers are seldom used in online documents. If possible, always try to identify the exact location of a source by using a section heading, a chapter, or a paragraph number if a page reference is not available. This is not an issue restricted to online sources because some traditional sources, such as speeches, interviews, and films do not use page numbers either.

Accuracy of URL details is essential for online documentation because a missing letter or punctuation mark may prevent a reader from accessing a web site. When entering URLs, always enclose them in angle brackets. URLs can be lengthy and it is often necessary to continue on a second line. In such a case, break the URL after a punctuation mark, such as a slash or a period. At all costs, **avoid hyphenating any split words.**

Otherwise you should follow the same procedures and principles for documenting your sources as explained earlier in this section. For example, you should follow similar procedures for repeat citations as explained on page 73.

The examples of online documentation shown on the following pages are based on the principles of the Chicago/Turabian style. As we explained earlier, this style of documentation comprises two components: a numbered footnote or endnote indicating the precise location of a quotation or idea, and a bibliography with details of the sources. The layout of the two components is similar except for the minor variations illustrated on page 74. We have provided the basic details of two online sources (a book and an article) for both a citation note and the bibliographic entry in shaded boxes. Immediately below each model we have demonstrated the documentation procedures with a specific example.

Footnotes/Endnotes

1. Author, *Title* (date of publication). <URL> [date of access], reference.

1. Noam Chomsky, *Rethinking Camelot: JFK, the Vietnam War, and U.S. Political Culture* (1993). <http://www.worldmedia.com/archive/rc/> [10 January 2000], 21.

2. Author, "Title of document," *Name of journal* volume/number (date of publication). <URL> [date of access], reference.

2. D. Menichetti, "German Policy in Occupied Belgium, 1914–1918," *Essays In History* 39 (1997). <http://etext.lib.virginia.edu/journals/EH/EH39/menich39.html> [11 January 2000], Conclusion.

Bibliography

Author. *Title*. Date of publication. <URL> [date of access].

Chomsky, Noam. *Rethinking Camelot: JFK, the Vietnam War, and U.S. Political Culture*. 1993. <http://www.worldmedia.com/archive/rc/> [10 January 2000].

Author. "Title of document." *Name of journal* volume/number. Date of publication. <URL> [date of access].

Menichetti, D. "German Policy in Occupied Belgium, 1914–1918." *Essays In History* 39. 1997. <http://etext.lib.virginia.edu/journals/EH/EH39/menich39.html> [11 January 2000].

CITING ONLINE SOURCES

REPORT

[1]Royal Commission on Aboriginal Peoples, *Royal Commission on Aboriginal Peoples — Final Report* (1996). <http://www.indigenus.bc.ca/rcap.htm> [26 January 2001], Introduction.

QUESTION AND ANSWER DATABASE

[2]*Soc.History.War.World-War-II Frequently Asked Questions* (n.d.). <http://www.cis.ohio-state.edu/hypertext/faq/usenet/world-war-2-faq/faq.html> [5 January 2001].

ENCYCLOPEDIA

[3]"League of Nations," *The Concise Columbia Electronic Encyclopedia*, 3rd ed. (1994). <http://www.encyclopedia.com/articles/07297.html> [12 January 2001], par.1.

NEWSPAPER ARTICLE

[4]Patrick Dare, "Enthused About the Art of an Essay," *The Ottawa Citizen* (7 January 1997). <http://www.ottawacitizen.com/ARCHIVE_1997/jan7/cit/cit2/cit2.html> [5 January 2000], par. 9.

NEWSLETTER

[5]Eric Hamilton, "Making Choices, Creating Opportunities," *History Now* (Spring 1997). <http://hss.cmu.edu/HTML/departments/history/Spring97_1.html> [12 January 2001].

ELECTRONIC JOURNAL OR MAGAZINE

[6]David Menichetti, "German Policy in Occupied Belgium, 1914–1918," *Essays In History* 39 (1997). <http://etext.lib.virginia.edu/journals/EH/EH39/menich39.html> [11 January 2001], Conclusion.

SLIDES/PHOTOGRAPHS

[7]The Simon Wiesenthal Center, *Neville Chamberlain with Adolf Hitler* (1997). <http://motlc.wiesenthal.com/gallery/pg18/pg7/pg18722.html> [5 January 2001].

MAP

[8]*The Axis Powers* 1942, map (n.d.). <http://www.indstate.edu/gga/gga_cart/78927.jpg> [5 January 2001].

SOUND

[9]Richard Millhouse Nixon, *Richard Nixon's Farewell Speech* [Sound file] (1974). <http://www.webcorp/sounds/nixonfar.au> [26 January 2001].

REVIEW (FILM OR BOOK)

[10]Gilbert Taylor, review of *Herschel: The Boy Who Started World War II*, by Andy Marino, *Booklist* (1 September 1997). <http://www.ala.org/booklist/v94/adult/se1/27marino.html> [12 January 2001].

TV/RADIO

[11]Mark O'Neill, "Chinese Traditional Medicines" [Sound file], *Quirks & Quarks* (23 May 1998). <http://www.radio.cbc.ca/programs/quirks/realaud/may2398.ra> [5 January 2001].

ART

[12]Emily Carr, *Kitseyucla* (c.1928). <http://www.mcmichael.on.ca/McMichael/carr-kitseyucla.jpg> [26 January 2001].

INTERVIEW

[13]Colin Bristow, interview by O. Bristow, *Local Heroes: An Oral History of World War Two* (n.d.). <http://www.localheroes.8m.com/cgi-bin/framed/2148/1.htm> [5 January 2001].

BOOK

[14]Robert F. Barsky, *Noam Chomskey: A Life of Dissent* (1997). <http://mitpress.mit.edu/e-books/chomsky/contents.html> [26 January 2001], 33.

ELECTRONIC MAIL

[15]Z. Arbenz <zarbenz@norwood.edu>, *League of Nations background* (12 January 2001). E-mail to Sue Conway <smconway@example.com>.

NEWSGROUP

[16]Henry Hillbrath <hillbrath@aol.com>, Re: *V2 launched from The Hague, Holland* <75ojf4$vi6$1@nntp6.u.washington.edu> (22 December 1998). <http://x15.dejanews.com/getdoc.xp?AN=424888357> [5 January 2001].

SOFTWARE PROGRAM

[17]*APA Style Helper*, Version 1.0. (1998). <http://www.apa.org/apa-style/> [5 January 2001].

PERSONAL WEB SITE

[18]Andrew Hunt, *Andrew's Diner* (n.d.). <http://www.arts.uwaterloo.ca/~aehunt/> [18 January 2001].

GENERAL WEB SITE

[19]The Modern Language Association of America, *MLA on the Web* (8 January 1999). <http://www.mla.org> [12 January 2001], MLA Style.

LISTING ONLINE SOURCES

REPORT

Royal Commission on Aboriginal Peoples. *Royal Commission on Aboriginal Peoples — Final Report*. 1996. <http://www.indigenous.bc.ca/rcap.htm> [26 January 2001].

QUESTION AND ANSWER DATABASE

Soc.History.War.World-War-II Frequently Asked Questions. N.d. <http://www.cis.ohio-state.edu/hypertext/faq/usenet/world-wr-2faq/faq.html> [5 January 2001].

ENCYCLOPEDIA

"League of Nations." *The Concise Columbia Electronic Encyclopedia*. 3rd ed. 1994. <http://www.encyclopedia.com/articles/07297.html> [12 January 2001].

NEWSPAPER ARTICLE

Dare, Patrick. "Enthused About the Art of an Essay." *The Ottawa Citizen*. 7 January 1997. <http://www.ottawacitizen.com/ARCHIVE_1997/jan7/cit/cit2/cit2.html> [5 January 2000].

NEWSLETTER

Hamilton, Eric. "Making Choices, Creating Opportunities." *History Now*. Spring 1997. <http://hss.cmu.edu/HTML/departments/history/Spring97_1.html> [12 January 2001].

ELECTRONIC JOURNAL OR MAGAZINE

Menichetti, D. "German Policy in Occupied Belgium, 1914–1918." *Essays In History* 39. 1997. <http://etext.lib.virginia.edu/journals/EH/EH39/menich39.html> [11 January 2001].

SLIDES/PHOTOGRAPHS

The Simon Wiesenthal Center. *Neville Chamberlain with Adolf Hitler*. 1997. <http://motlc.wiesenthal.com/gallery/pg18/pg7/pg18722.html> [5 January 2001].

MAP

The Axis Powers 1942. Map. N.d. <http://www.indstate.edu/gga/gga_cart/78927.jpg> [5 January 2001].

SOUND

Nixon, Richard Millhouse. *Richard Nixon's Farewell Speech* [Sound file]. 1974. <http://www.webcorp.com/sounds/nixonfar.au> [26 January 2001].

REVIEW (FILM OR BOOK)

Taylor, Gilbert. Review of Herschel: *The Boy Who Started World War II*, by Andy Marino. *Booklist*. 1 September 1997.<http://www.ala.org/booklist/v94/adult/se1/27marino. html> [12 January 2001].

TV/RADIO

O'Neill, Mark. "Chinese Traditional Medicines" [Sound file]. *Quirks & Quarks*. 23 May 1998. <http://www.radio.cbc.ca/ programs/quirks/realaud/may2398.ra> [5 January 2001].

ART

Carr, Emily. *Kitseyucla*. c.1928. <http://www.mcmichael.on.ca/ McMichael/carr-kitseyucla.jpg> [26 January 2001].

INTERVIEW

Bristow, Colin. Interview by O. Bristow. *Local Heroes: An Oral History of World War Two* N.d. <http://www.localheroes. 8m.com/cgi-bin/framed/2148/1.htm> [5 January 2001].

BOOK

Barsky, Robert F. *Noam Chomsky: A Life of Dissent.* 1997. <http://www.mitpress.mit.edu/e-books/chomsky/contents. html> [26 January 2001].

ELECTRONIC MAIL

Arbenz, Z. <zarbenz@norwood.edu>. *League of Nations background.* 12 January 2001. E-mail to Sue Conway <smconway@example.com>.

NEWSGROUP

Hillbrath, Henry <hillbrath@aol.com>. Re: *V2 launched from The Hague, Holland.* <75ojf4$vi6$1@nntp6.u.washington. edu> 22 December 1998. <http://x15.dejanews.com/ getdoc.xp?AN=424888357> [5 January 2001].

SOFTWARE PROGRAM

APA Style Helper. Version 1.0. 1998. <http://www.apa.org/ apa-style/> [5 January 2001].

PERSONAL WEB SITE

Hunt, Andrew. *Andrew's Diner.* N.d. <http://www.arts.uwaterloo.ca/ ~aehunt/> [18 January 2001].

GENERAL WEB SITE

The Modern Language Association of America. *MLA on the Web.* 1997. <http://www.mla.org> [12 January 2001].

The list of sources for the League of Nations essay laid out in the Chicago/Turabian style is shown below.

Works Consulted

Barros, James. *Office without Power*. Oxford: Clarendon Press, 1979.

Baer, George W. *Test Case: Italy, Ethiopia, and the League of Nations*. Stanford: Hoover Institution Press, 1976.

The Covenant of the League of Nations. *The Versailles Treaty*. 28 June 1919. <http://acusd.edu/History/text/versaillestreaty/ver001.html> [1 January 2001].

Egerton, George W. *Great Britain and the Creation of the League of Nations*. Chapel Hill, NC: University of North Carolina Press, 1978.

_____. "Collective Security as Political Myth: Liberal Internationalism and The League of Nations in Politics and History." *International History Review* 5 (1983): 496-524.

Kennedy, Paul. "Appeasement." In *The Origins of the Second World War Reconsidered: The A.J.P. Taylor Debate after Twenty-five Years*, ed. Gordon Martel. Boston: Allen and Unwin, 1986.

League of Nations. *League of Nations Armament Yearbook, 1939-1940*. 1940. <http://www.library.nwu.edu/govpub/collections/league/arms-yrbook/1939-40> [1 January 2001].

Margulies, H.F. "The Moderates in the League of Nations' Battle; An Overlooked Faction." *Historian* 60 (1998): 273-287.

Northedge, F.S. *The League of Nations: Its Life and Times, 1920-1946*. Leicester: Leicester University Press, 1986.

Walters, F.P. *A History of the League of Nations*. Oxford: Oxford University Press, 1952.

Explanatory Notes

Documentation involves **citing in text** by numbered reference to a footnote or endnote and **listing the sources** at the end of the essay. There is another type of note that has a different function to the citation (or documentary) footnote or endnote. The explanatory note is used for additional information that, while relevant to the essay, could detract from the development of your argument if inserted directly in the text. For example, it may be necessary to provide additional biographical information on a person. Translations, definitions, and alternative viewpoints can also be placed in explanatory notes.

Although explanatory information can either be placed in footnotes or in endnotes, it is more convenient for the reader to refer to explanatory information at the bottom of the page than to turn to the end of the essay. **If you are using endnotes to cite your sources**, you can identify items requiring explanation by assigning asterisks (*) or other symbols (†) in the text and linking them to corresponding symbols in footnotes. For an example of an explanatory footnote, see page 8 of this guide. **If you are using footnotes to cite your sources**, do not combine symbols (for explanatory information) and numbers (for citing sources). It is simpler and clearer to use one set of superscript numbers for both citation notes and explanatory notes.

You must resist the temptation to place too much information in explanatory notes because constant reference to footnotes or endnotes may distract the reader from the development of your argument. Ask yourself whether the information is essential to the essay. If not, eliminate it. If it is, consider incorporating the information in the text before creating an explanatory note. In the case of lengthy information, consider placing it in the appendix instead of creating a note. Whichever method you use for explanatory material, it is important that you strive for **consistency, simplicity, and clarity**.

Explanatory notes are not part of the citation procedure, but they are used in close conjunction with it. Therefore, it is especially important to determine whether the purpose of each note is to cite a source or to provide explanation.

Author-Date

Citing Sources

Another method of acknowledging and identifying your sources is to provide the author's last name, the date of publication of the work, and a page reference in a parenthetical citation in the text of your essay, as follows:

The lack of any binding commitment on the part of League members was a major factor in its downfall (Northedge, 1986, 51).

The reader can then refer to the list of sources at the end of the essay to obtain complete bibliographic details. In the list of sources, the reference would be entered as follows:

Northedge, F.S. (1986). *The League of Nations: Its life and times, 1920–1946.* **Leicester: Leicester University Press.**

The in-text procedure enables the reader to determine the sources quickly, but frequent parenthetical citations tend to disrupt the fluency of the text. Include just the essential citations. Improve readability by placing the citation at the end of a sentence or where a pause occurs, such as a punctuation mark, and include the author's name in the text if possible, as shown below.

Economist Janine Velasquez (2000) argues that "floating exchange rates facilitate global trade" (49).

For further examples, refer to the sample League of Nations essay on pages 47 and 48. Always attempt to specify the exact location of information by using a page reference. Some of the more common forms of parenthetical citations using the author-date system are shown on the next page. These examples are based largely on the procedures in the *Publication Manual* of the American Psychological Association (APA). Only the in-text parenthetical citations are provided here; corresponding entries in the list of sources (References or Works Consulted) at the end of the essay are shown separately on pages 92–95.

Citing a work by two authors:

Strunk and White (1979) recommend avoiding the use of qualifiers (73).

Citing a work by three to five authors:

First citation: Jackson, North, Hill, and Cruz (1998) discovered that . . .

Subsequent citations: Jackson et al. (1998) argue that . . .

Citing a work by six or more authors:

Hazen et al. (1993, 101) describe how . . .

Citing a work by a corporate author:

The Committee on Famine Relief (1997) reports that agricultural practices have exacerbated the plight of refugees (9–10).

Citing a work with no author:

The Chicago Manual of Style (1993) offers an alternative documentation system.

The rival parties showed no inclination to compromise ("Discordant accord," 1998,10).

Citing multiple works within the same parentheses:

American volunteers participated in the Boer War for different reasons (Strong, 1963, 7; Williams, 1971, 49).

Citing a multivolume work with a page reference:

Strindberg's complex dramatic structure is perfectly expressive of another key expressionistic idea: the illusory quality of time and space (Gassner, 1980, 2:780).

Citing a work with no date of publication:

In an interesting account published during the Depression (Preston, n.d.) . . .

Citing indirect sources:

Curtis' explanation (cited in Pakenham, 1979) differs from . . .

Listing Sources

Brief in-text parenthetical citations have to be linked to a list of sources containing complete bibliographic details at the end of the essay. It is common practice in the author-date system for the list of sources to reflect only those **sources cited in the essay.** A list of cited sources is titled "References," although alternative terms such as "Sources Cited" or "Works Cited" are usually acceptable.

On the other hand, your instructor may ask you to provide a list of **all the sources that proved useful** in preparing the essay, even if you did not cite all of them directly. If you included both useful sources and cited sources, you may designate your list either "Works Consulted" or "Bibliography." "References" can also be used to cover this category of sources.

"Bibliography" is still a widely used term, but some instructors object to it on two counts. First, the word "bibliography" literally means a " list of books," and sources today range from books to interviews to databases. Second, "bibliography" implies a complete list of sources on a topic, and student sources for an essay are unlikely to represent an exhaustive list. Consider using "Select Bibliography" as an alternative designation.

Whatever procedure you choose, your sources should be listed in alphabetical order by author's last name in a separate section at the end of the essay. **Do not number your sources.** Use a single list of sources for high school and university essays. For longer research papers and dissertations you may be required to classify your sources into primary and secondary material, published and unpublished information, or cited references and additional sources. The classified structure of the Working Bibliography recommended earlier in this guide suggested that sources be grouped under headings such as "Books," "Articles," and "Audio-Visual." This division was to encourage a diversity of sources. The final list of sources should not be grouped in this manner.

The entry for each source starts at the left margin, with the author's last name listed first, followed by the initials or first names. Next, the publication date of the work is placed in parentheses. The title of the work follows the publication date. In the author-date system it is customary to capitalize only the first word of the title and of the subtitle and any proper nouns. Some instructors may prefer the standard method of capitalization. Publication details complete the entry. If an entry extends beyond one line, the second and subsequent lines are indented three spaces, or alternatively use a tab space or paragraph indent. Entries may be single or double-spaced, but double-spacing is required between individual references.

If there is no place of publication given, use "N.p." and for no publisher use "n.p." If both are missing, it is permissible to use just "N.p." If no date is provided, insert "n.d." in parentheses. Abbreviations are commonly used in the author-date system. For example, initials often replace personal names, and descriptions of publishing companies may be simplified, such as "Oxford UP" in place of "Oxford University Press."

You may be required to make descriptive or critical comments on the merits of each source, as shown below. In such a case, head your list of sources "Annotated References."

Dunham, Aileen. (1963). *Political Unrest in Upper Canada, 1815–1836*. Toronto: McLelland and Stewart.

A detailed study of the underlying political events that led to the rebellion in Upper Canada in 1837. It is most useful for an understanding of the political problems of the period. Although dated, it is certainly not an outdated work.

Shown on the following pages are examples of how to list the more common types of sources. These samples are based largely on the procedures described in the APA *Publication Manual*. Consult the manual for further details and more specialized forms, but bear in mind that the *Publication Manual* is directed primarily at researchers preparing articles for publication. Therefore, it is especially important to clarify citation and reference procedures with your instructor before starting your essay. Furthermore, APA style, although widely used, is only one of a number of author-date systems.

BOOK

ONE AUTHOR

Johnston, Alastair Iain. (1995). *Cultural realism: Strategic culture and grand strategy in Chinese history.* Princeton: Princeton UP.

TWO AUTHORS

Blight, James and Welch, David. (1989). *On the brink: Americans and Soviets reexamine the Cuban Missile Crisis.* New York: Hill & Wang.

MORE THAN THREE AUTHORS/EDITORS

Brown, J., Manning, P., Shapiro, K., and Wiener, J. (1991). *History from South Africa: Alternative visions and practices.* Philadelphia: Temple University Press.

EDITOR/COMPILER/TRANSLATOR

Krueger, Anne. (Ed). (1998). T*he WTO as an international organization.* Chicago: University of Chicago Press.

NO AUTHOR

Beowulf. Wright, David. (Trans.). (1960). Harmondsworth, U.K: Penguin. (Do not use "Anonymous" or "Anon.")

CORPORATE AUTHOR

American Psychological Association. (1994). *Publication manual* (4th ed.). Washington, DC: Author.

MULTIVOLUME WORK

Durant, Will and Ariel. (1960–1965). *The story of civilization: Vol. 10. Rousseau and revolution* (201–220). New York: Simon and Schuster.

ESSAY IN AN EDITED WORK

Wrigley, Christopher. (1976). Changes in East African society. In D.A. Low and Alison Smith (Eds.), *A history of East Africa* (500–520). Oxford: Oxford University Press.

LATER EDITION

van Leunen, Mary-Claire. (1992). *A handbook for scholars* (Rev. ed.). New York: Oxford UP.

PAMPHLET/MONOGRAPH

Lacasse, Danielle and Lechasseur, Antonio. (1997). *The National Archives of Canada, 1872–1997* (Historical Booklet 58). Ottawa: Canadian Historical Association.

OTHER LANGUAGE

Kosok, Heinz. (1960). *Geschichte der anglo-irischen literatur* [A history of Anglo-Irish literature]. Berlin: Erich Schmidt.

ENCYCLOPEDIA

Jones, Manfred. (1978). Isolationism. In *The encyclopedia of American foreign policy* (2:496–506).   New York: Charles Scribner.

YEARBOOK

Yapko, Michael D. (1996). Repressed memories: Special report. *Britannica book of the year* 1995 (198–199). Chicago: Encyclopaedia Britannica.

NEWSPAPER

ARTICLE

Baxter, Duncan. (1999, January 1). Generation soundbite. *Times* (London).

EDITORIAL

Discordant accord. (1998, December 28). [Editorial]. *Times of India*.

LETTER TO THE EDITOR

Traister, Bryce. (1999, January 16). Free speech at university [Letter to the editor]. *Globe and Mail* (Toronto).

OBITUARY

Allen, William. (1999, January 1). [Obituary]. *Times* (London).

MAGAZINE

SIGNED ARTICLE

Rahman, Gideon. (1993, April 17). Indonesia: A survey.   *The Economist*, 3–18.

UNSIGNED ARTICLE

Quark hunters. (1990, October 29). *Time*, 36–37.

JOURNAL

CONTINUOUS PAGINATION

Claude, I.L. (1981). Casual commitment to international relations. *Political Science Quarterly,96*, 367–79.

SEPARATE PAGINATION

Feldstein, Martin. (1998). Refocusing the IMF. *Foreign Affairs,77* (2), 20–33.

NEWSLETTER

Reid, John. (1990). Historians and the National Archives of Canada. *Bulletin of the Canadian Historical Association, 16* (4), 5–12.

REVIEW

BOOK

Appiah, Anthony. (1998, December 17). Africa: The hidden history [Review of the book *Africa: A biography of the continent*]. *New York Review of Books*, 64–72.

FILM

Ansen, David. (1990, November 19). How the west was lost [Review of the film *Dances with wolves*]. *Newsweek*, 67–68.

INTERVIEW

PERSONAL

McCormick, Edwin. (1980, January 10). [Interview by author]. Toronto, Ontario.

PUBLISHED

Gordimer, Nadine. (1991, October 14). The power of a well-told tale [Interview by P. Gray and B. Nelan]. *Time*, 92–93.

RADIO/TELEVISION

Gordimer, Nadine. (1991, May 26). [Interview by Eleanor Wachtel]. *Writers and Company*. CBC Stereo.

CONFERENCE PAPER (UNPUBLISHED)

Fodrea, Jim. (1998). *Pacific north west salmon reservoir operation issues*. Paper presented at the International Water Resources Engineering Conference, Reston, VA.

DISSERTATION

UNPUBLISHED

Robertson, Justin L. (1998). Strategic industrial sectors in the world trading system: The case of Indonesia. Unpublished master's thesis, Dalhousie University, Halifax, Canada.

ABSTRACT

Shimko, Keith L. (1990). Images and policy debates. (Doctoral dissertation, Indiana University, 1990). *Dissertation Abstracts International* 51A, 1766 A.

SPEECH/LECTURE

Peck, M. Scott. (1990, September 22). *A new psychology of love, traditional values, and spiritual growth* [Lecture]. The Centre of New Fire. Ottawa, Canada.

FILM

Costner, Kevin. (Director). (1990). *Dances with wolves* [Film]. Los Angeles: TIG/Orion.

VIDEOCASSETTE

Burns, Ken. (Director). (1994). *The civil war* [Videocassette]. New York: PBS.

RADIO/TELEVISION PROGRAM

Morris, Desmond. (Narrator). (1999, January 15). The human zoo. In *The human animal*. New York: The Learning Channel.

WORK OF ART

Picasso, Pablo. (1912). *Still life with chair-caning* [Oil on canvas]. Musée Picasso, Paris.

SOUND RECORDING

Shakespeare,William. *Twelfth night*. (1961). (Howard Sackler, Director). [Cassette]. New York: Caedmon.

MAP

Physical United States. (1997). [Map]. Washington, DC: National Geographic.

PUBLIC DOCUMENT

U.S. Library of Congress. (1997). *Annual report of the Librarian of Congress, 1997*. Washington, DC: Government Printing Office.

MANUSCRIPT

Hare, W.A. (1900). [Papers]. National Archives, Ottawa, Canada.

CD-ROM

Discover the Great Lakes: The ecosystem of the Great Lakes-St. Lawrence. (1997). [CD-ROM]. Ottawa: Environment Canada.

INDIRECT SOURCE

Pakenham, Thomas. (1979). *The Boer war* (101). London: Weidenfeld and Nicholson. Citing L. Curtis. (1951). *With Milner in South Africa* (87). Oxford: Oxford University Press.

Certain elements in these entries have been italicized. If you are writing with a word processor, italicize these elements. In typed essays, elements italicized in these examples should be underlined. Two or more sources by the same author are listed in chronological order of publication. See Egerton in the sample References on page 99.

Online Sources

Like print or video sources used in an essay, online material must also be documented. As explained on pages 114–117, there are major differences between traditional sources and online sources. Some of these differences directly influence documentation procedures.

Online sources are ephemeral — they may exist today and disappear tomorrow. Online sources are frequently updated and they can be easily modified by adding or deleting details. Furthermore, the access route and the address or URL may change. Because of their fleeting nature and ease of alteration, it is necessary to provide **two dates when citing online sources** — the date of publication or latest revision and the date that you consulted the source.

Since sources frequently disappear or change drastically, you may wish to print copies of your online sources or alternatively save them to disk as confirmation of their existence, brief as it sometimes is. Consider printing just the first page of lengthy documents as proof of their existence.

In printed sources, such as a book, a page reference in a citation note indicates the specific location of important material used in the essay. But page numbers are seldom used in online documents. If possible, always try to identify the exact location of a source by using a section heading, a chapter, or a paragraph number if a page reference is not available. This is not an issue restricted to online sources because some traditional sources, such as speeches, interviews, and films do not use page numbers either.

Accuracy of URL details is essential for online documentation because a missing letter or punctuation mark may prevent a reader from accessing a web site. When entering URLs, always enclose them in angle brackets. URLs can be lengthy and it is often necessary to continue on a second line. In such a case, break the URL after a punctuation mark, such as a slash or a period. At all costs, **avoid hyphenating any split words.**

Otherwise you should follow the same procedures and principles for documenting your sources as explained earlier in this section. For example, you should follow similar procedures for citing in text, as explained on pages 88-89.

REPORT

Royal Commission on Aboriginal Peoples. (1996). *Royal Commission on Aboriginal Peoples — Final Report.* <http://www.indigenous.bc.ca/rcap.htm> [2001, January 26].

QUESTION AND ANSWER DATABASE

Soc.history.war.World-War-II frequently asked questions. (N.d.). <http://www.cis.ohio-state.edu/hypertext/faq/usenet/world-war-2-faq/faq.html> [2001, January 5].

ENCYCLOPEDIA

League of Nations. (1994). In *The concise Columbia electronic encyclopedia* (3rd ed.). <http://www.encyclopedia.com/articles/07297.html> [2001, January 12].

NEWSPAPER ARTICLE

Dare, Patrick. (1997, January 7). Enthused about the art of an essay. *The Ottawa Citizen.* <http://www.ottawacitizen.com/ARCHIVE_1997/jan7/cit/cit2/cit2.html> [2000, January 5].

NEWSLETTER

Hamilton, Eric. (Spring 1997). Making choices, creating opportunities. *History Now.* <http://hss.cmu.edu/HTML/departments/history/Spring97_1.html> [2001, January 12].

ELECTRONIC JOURNAL OR MAGAZINE

Menichetti, David. (1997). German policy in occupied Belgium, 1914–1918. *Essays In History, 39.* <http://etext.lib.virginia.edu/journals/EH/EH39/menich39.html> [2001, January 11].

SLIDES/PHOTOGRAPHS

The Simon Wiesenthal Center. (1997). *Neville Chamberlain with Adolf Hitler* [Photograph]. <http://motlc.wiesenthal.com/gallery/pg18/pg7/pg18722.html> [2001, January 5].

MAP

The Axis powers 1942. (N.d.). [Map].<http://www.indstate.edu/gga/gga_cart/78927.jpg> [2001, January 5].

SOUND

Nixon, Richard Millhouse. (1974). *Richard Nixon's farewell speech* [Sound file]. <http://www.webcorp.com/sounds/nisonfar.au> [2001, January 26].

REVIEW (FILM OR BOOK)

Taylor, Gilbert. (1997, September 1). [Review of the book *Herschel: The boy who started World War II*]. *Booklist.* <http://www.ala.org/booklist/v94/adult/se1/27marino.html> [2001, January 12].

TV/Radio
O'Neill, Mark. (1998, May 23). Chinese traditional medicines [Sound file]. *Quirks & Quarks*. <http://www.radio.cbc.ca/programs/quirks/realaud/may2398.ra> [2001, January 5].

Art
Carr, Emily. (c.1928). *Kitseyucla*. <http://www.mcmichael.on.ca/McMichael/carr-kitseyucla.jpg> [2001, January 26].

Interview
Bristow, Colin. (N.d.). [Interviewed by Owen Bristow]. *Local heroes: An oral history of World War Two*. <http://www.localheroes.8m.com/cgi-bin/framed/2148/1.htm> [2001, January 5].

Book
Barsky, Robert F. (1997). *Noam Chomsky: A Life of Dissent*. <http://mitpress.mit.edu.e-books/chomsky/contents.html> [2001, January 26].

Electronic Mail
Arbenz, Z. <zarbenz@norwood.edu> (2001, February 1). *League of Nations background*. E-mail to Sue Conway <smconway@example.com>.

Newsgroup
Hillbrath, Henry <hillbrath@aol.com> (1998, December 22). Re: V2 launched from The Hague, Holland. <75ojf4$vi6$1@nntp6.u.washington.edu> <http://x15.dejanews.com/getdoc.xp?AN=424888357> [2001, 5 January].

Software Program
APA style helper (Version 1.0.). (1998). <http://www.apa.org/apa-style/> [2001, January 5].

Personal Web Site
Hunt, Andrew. (N.d.). *Andrew's diner*. <http://www.arts.uwaterloo.ca/~aehunt/> [2001, January 18].

General Web Site
The Modern Language Association of America. (1999, January 8). *MLA on the Web*. <http://www.mla.org> [2001, January 12].

The list of sources for the League of Nations essay laid out in APA style is shown below.

References

Barros, James. (1979). *Office without power.* Oxford: Clarendon Press.

Baer, George W. (1976). *Test case: Italy, Ethiopia, and the League of Nations.* Stanford: Hoover Institution Press.

The Covenant of the League of Nations. (1919, June 28). *The Versailles Treaty.* <http://ac.acusd.edu/History/text/versaillestreaty/ver001.html> [2001, February 1].

Egerton, George W. (1978). *Great Britain and the creation of the League of Nations.* Chapel Hill, NC: University of North Carolina Press.

Egerton, George W. (1983). Collective security as political myth: Liberal internationalism and the League of Nations in politics and history. *International History Review, 5,* 496–524.

Kennedy, Paul. (1986). Appeasement. In Gordon Martel (Ed.), *The origins of the Second World War reconsidered: The A.J.P. Taylor debate after twenty-five years* (140–161). Boston: Allen and Unwin.

League of Nations. (1940). *League of Nations Armament Yearbook, 1939–40.* <http://www.library.nwu.edu/govpub/collections/league/arms-yrbook/1939-40> [2001, February 1].

Margulies, H.F. (1998, Winter). The moderates in the League of Nations' battle: An overlooked faction. *Historian, 60,* 273–287.

Northedge, F.S. (1986). *The League of Nations: Its life and times, 1920–1946.* Leicester: Leicester University Press.

Walters, F.P. (1952). *A history of the League of Nations.* Oxford: Oxford University Press.

Explanatory Notes

Sometimes it is necessary to include information which, while relevant to the essay, could detract from the development of your argument if inserted directly into the text. For example, it may be necessary to provide additional biographical information on a person. This information can be isolated in a separate explanatory note. Translations and definitions may also be placed in explanatory notes.

Identify an item requiring explanation by using a superscript number in the text. Then write the note after the corresponding number either at the bottom of the page as a footnote or on a separate page at the end of the essay as an endnote. Notes are numbered consecutively throughout the essay.

Footnotes are separated from the text by a solid line twenty spaces in length. Leave a blank line and then indent five spaces or a tab stop. Type the number in superscript followed by the note. If the note continues beyond one line, start subsequent lines at the left margin. Single space any notes that continue on a second line, but leave a double space between individual notes. Use a slightly smaller font size for your footnotes than the regular type used in the essay.

Another method is to place all your explanatory notes in a separate section at the end of the essay just before the list of sources. Title the page "Notes" and enter the details as explained above for footnotes. For endnotes you may double-space throughout and use the same font size as you used in the essay.

You must resist the temptation to place too much information in explanatory notes because constant reference to footnotes or endnotes may distract the reader from the development of your argument. Ask yourself whether the information is essential to the essay. If not, eliminate it. If it is, consider incorporating the information in the text before creating an explanatory note. In the case of lengthy information, consider placing it in the appendix instead of creating a note.

Always consult with your instructor about the need for explanatory information and where you should place it. But whichever method you use, it is important that you strive for **consistency, simplicity, and clarity.**

STYLE

Style is the manner of your writing rather than the substance of your essay. It is the written expression of your ideas, not the ideas themselves, or as Lucile Payne puts it: "It is the 'how' (form) as opposed to the 'what' (content)."[14] Every person's writing style is unique. Although your style reflects your personality, your style must still be governed by the conventions of language usage. You cannot adopt a style that departs drastically from orthodox sentence structure and commonly accepted forms of punctuation if you wish to communicate successfully. Many manuals have been published on English usage and writing style. This book does not claim to be a style manual. However, this section does offer some practical tips on how to become proficient at the craft of writing essays and thereby shape a clear and smooth personal style.

Reading

Read as many books and magazines as you can. Read widely, from the classics to contemporary literature. If you find a particular piece of writing effective, try to determine why it is effective. If you encounter new words, as you undoubtedly will, add them to your vocabulary. Reading the editorials in reputable newspapers and magazines is good training for essay writing, since editorials are often mini-essays with arguments based on evidence. Remember that reading, writing, and thinking are inseparably linked.

Writing

Experiment with the different writing techniques that you have identified through your reading. Writing is not an innate gift — it is a craft that must be learned. Like sports stars and chess players, good writers develop their craft through practice and persistence. As with most skills, cultivating successful style is usually only ten percent inspiration and ninety percent perspiration.

Clarity

Clarity of expression is one of the key features of a successful style. Brevity, simplicity, and precision are the essential qualities of clear style. Prune ruthlessly as you edit your draft and eliminate the clutter of foggy phrases such as "at that point in time" or "by the same token."[15] "Etcetera/ (etc.)" is a meaningless term and should never be used.

Vocabulary

Judicious selection of words not only ensures clarity of meaning, it also enhances the sound and harmony of your writing. Always choose concrete words over vague terms and abstract generalizations in your writing. A reputable dictionary and a thesaurus or dictionary of synonyms are essential companions for a writer.

Fluency

Good writing has an even flow. Give your writing rhythm and harmony by your choice of words and your use of punctuation. For instance, you can use transitional words such as "nevertheless," "consequently," and "furthermore" to link the flow of ideas; and you can use punctuation structures — such as a series of clauses linked by semi-colons — to present your ideas to their best advantage. Test your writing for eloquence by reading it aloud and then fine-tune it until it flows smoothly and naturally.

Tone

An essay is a work of ideas, not moods or feelings and therefore, it must have a formal and scholarly tone. Contractions such as "can't" and "won't" should not be used in formal writing, even though they are part of everyday speech. Likewise, slang, jargon, and trendy, overused expressions, such as "prioritize," have no place in an essay.

Jargon

Every academic discipline has its own jargon and code words. Some of these words are necessary and useful, since they can define a concept with great precision, but some of them are no more than big words designed to impress a reader. These words usually obscure the meaning of the essay. A good essay is not something written in a secret code that only the writer and the instructor can understand; a good essay should be accessible to any intelligent reader.

Discriminatory Language

Never use language that discriminates on the grounds of sex, race, or religion. Language that stereotypes people and groups is unacceptable in any type of writing. In particular, avoid using the masculine pronoun when referring to human groups that could legitimately be male or female, or comprised of both sexes. Guides are available to help you substitute words that are free of discrimination.

Pronouns

Instructors do not agree on the use of pronouns in essays. Some accept the use of the first person "I," others reject its use. Some prefer "the author" or "the writer," while others regard these terms as pretentious. "We" or "one" find acceptance with some instructors, but not with others. However, there is near unanimity on avoiding the use of the second person pronoun "you" in formal academic writing. ("You" is used frequently in this book because it is an instructional manual.) Always clarify the preferences of your instructors about the use of pronouns.

Punctuation

Pay attention to punctuation. Good punctuation can improve the readability and clarity of your essay to a remarkable degree. Since an essay is a formal piece of writing, do not use the exclamation mark and minimize the use of the dash.

Grammar

Language is based on rules and conventions that serve to clarify comprehension. If you ignore rules and conventions, you will only obscure the meaning of your essay. Develop a sound knowledge of basic grammar and do not simply rely on a computer grammar check program.

Sentences

Vary the length of your sentences to change the pace of your writing. Shorter sentences can be used to give emphasis to a point. Further emphasis can be given by placing the key words at the end of the sentence. Make sure that every sentence really is a sentence, with a proper subject and a verb.

Verbs

Research papers are usually written in the past tense. But writing in the past tense does not mean that you should adopt a "passive" sentence structure. Use active verbs to give force to your writing. Do not say, "Napoleon was beaten at the battle of Waterloo by Wellington" when you can say, "Wellington defeated Napoleon at the battle of Waterloo." Guard against an increasing tendency to use nouns as verbs. For example, "impact" and "dialogue" are nouns, not verbs — "to impact" and "to dialogue" do not exist.

Spelling

Careless spelling can mar an otherwise well-written essay. Use a dictionary and the spell check function on the computer to correct errors. No spelling errors should slip through the final proofreading.

Paragraphs

Remember the importance of paragraphs. They reflect the structure of your essay and structure is a key component of clarity.

❖ ❖ ❖

A pleasing style is not based solely on rigid and mechanically correct English. Attempt to breathe vigour and vitality into your writing. Do not be discouraged if your first efforts do not create the effects that you want: developing a good writing style requires dedication and application, effort and practice. But the payoff is worth it, for a pleasing style will not only enhance the clarity of your essay, it will also add a persuasive element to your arguments. **More importantly, a lucid writing style is a lifelong asset.**

CONCLUSION

Each essay is an exploration into unknown territory. Like all journeys of discovery you will experience both elation and tribulation, fascination and frustration. The excitement of probing problems and developing new insights will frequently be offset by the difficulties of meeting deadlines, structuring arguments, and crafting ideas into words. There is no "quick fix" formula for preparing quality assignments. But with practice, patience, and enthusiasm you will overcome the obstacles that you encounter.

There are methods and procedures for research and writing in the humanities and social sciences; the preparation of a good essay is not a mystery. This manual has outlined a method that follows a systematic and logical progression from the first step of selecting a topic through to the final submission of the completed assignment. It is a flexible model; you may wish to modify it and shape your own process. No matter what method you develop, it is important to have an organized approach for processing information and communicating your ideas.

We live in an age of escalating volumes of information. While it is important to have a process to locate and organize this wealth of information, it is the less tangible and the less technical skills associated with the process that will be more important in the long run. These skills include the depth and precision of your thinking: for example, creative thinking, such as brainstorming novel insights and generating imaginative ideas; critical thinking, such as evaluating your sources and assessing arguments; and logical thinking, such as constructing a clear and convincing thesis.

Reading, writing, and discussion help to develop and sharpen all types of thinking. As well-known writer E.M. Forster reminds us: how do we know what we think until we see what we have written? Therefore, you also need to have a proficient command of the language to express with clarity and precision the thoughts and ideas generated by your research.

Use computer technology to supplement and enhance the more traditional, and almost timeless, techniques described in this manual. But use the technology judiciously, because the computer is only a tool — it will not think for you.

In mastering the techniques of researching and writing, you will have cultivated a valuable set of skills and acquired a personal sense of satisfaction that only creative activity can bring. Such talents will serve you well throughout life.

Appendix

1. Research Aids

Computers facilitate the research process by providing access to local databases, the Internet, and CD-ROM databases.

- Most libraries have replaced their card catalogues with databases of computer-readable records accessible through terminals onsite. These **local** or internal databases contain details of each library's holdings.

- The explosion of the **Internet** enables researchers to search resources around the world with ease and speed. These online or external resources comprise both full-text material, such as newspapers, as well as bibliographic citation databases, such as periodical indexes.

- Many databases are available in **CD-ROM** format. Like Internet resources, CD-ROM versions provide both full-text sources and searching capabilities. CD-ROM databases are available through networked systems or stand-alone stations in many libraries.

Information technology, while offering exciting opportunities for researchers, also contains potential pitfalls. The Internet is not a library; it is more like a gigantic electronic bookstore where not only are the titles listed, but the contents of many documents are also available. Library resources and catalogues are compiled by specialists, whereas searches on the Internet usually return sources compiled by a computer program. As a result, the classification of online material is often inconsistent and haphazard. Therefore, you may score thousands of "hits," many irrelevant, when doing a keyword search.

There are other limitations, such as copyright, which restrict the number of quality "publications" available on the Internet. Another limitation is that access to some of the best databases is restricted by the information providers to those who pay fees. The Internet does offer free material, but much of it is of dubious quality.

Despite these limitations, computers provide some distinct advantages for developing a comprehensive Working Bibliography. Besides speedy access to material, you can search by keyword or use Boolean logic to narrow your search. Many search engines also have help pages with advice on research methods. Libraries often have web sites listing resources that have been compiled by specialists. Some sites, devoted to academic topics and authors, are maintained by professors and librarians.

Since cyberspace is an environment in constant flux, it is impossible to provide current and comprehensive details on using the Internet. Consult guides such as *Online!*, or speak to librarians, and check web sites that offer practical advice. Remember, however, that the Internet is only one tool in your kit of research skills.

Computer techniques can complement traditional searching methods. In some instances the two overlap. For example, many printed works, such as books and encyclopedias, are available on both CD-ROM and online. In other areas the two formats have each developed their own niche. For example, many printed works will never be digitized because of copyright restrictions, while many online documents are never printed because they become dated quickly or because of cost. While most indexes are produced in electronic form today, the early volumes are usually only available in print. When searching for sources, use strategies that include both traditional methods and the latest technology.

On the following pages you will find a comprehensive list of research aids. These resources are supplemented with examples that may be in formats as varied as print, microform, audio-visual, online, or CD-ROM. For additional information on searching methods and for a discussion of the merits of the "real" and the "virtual" library, there is no better resource to consult than Thomas Mann's excellent guide, which is listed in the Works Consulted on page 153.

- The catalogue is the main source of information about the library's resources. Computer catalogues offer greater versatility for searching than the traditional author/title and subject divisions of the card system. For example, you can search by a keyword in the title. Enter the term "imperialism" and the computer will list all works with "imperialism" in the title regardless of the position of the word.

- Since the richness of language usually permits a concept to be expressed in a number of different ways, it is possible that subject terms familiar to you may not be the ones selected by the author for the title. In order to help you find works on the same subject, the Library of Congress devised the *Library of Congress Subject Headings (LCSH)*. If you look up the term "Diplomacy" in the *LCSH*, for example, you will find a number of related headings that you can use in your searching.

- Although it may seem old-fashioned in the age of computer technology, browsing can be an effective means of expanding your list of sources. You can locate your "browsing area" in the library by using the *LCSH* and the catalogue to determine which stacks hold books on your topic. By running your eye along the shelves you will often discover useful sources. And by checking tables of contents and indexes you will often pinpoint pertinent information in sources that would not be revealed in a catalogue search. A careful scrutiny of bibliographies and references in books on related topics will often turn up additional sources.

- The reference shelves, containing a wide assortment of material, can be an especially profitable area for browsing.
    Atlases, e.g. *Atlas of Ancient Archaeology*
    Almanacs, e.g. *The World Almanac and Book of Facts*
    Yearbooks, e.g. *Urban History Yearbook*
    Handbooks, e.g. *Handbook of Latin American Studies*
    Research Guides, e.g. *Research Guide to Philosophy*
    Chronologies, e.g. *World Chronology of Music History*
    Dictionaries, e.g. *Dictionary of American Art*
    Encyclopedias, e.g. *Encyclopedia of Crime and Justice*

Encyclopedias can be general, such as the *Encyclopaedia Britannica*, or specific, such as *The Encyclopedia of*

American Foreign Policy. You can gain access to many specialized encyclopedias by consulting *First Stop: The Master Index to Subject Encyclopedias* or similar indexes. There are published guides, classified by subject areas, that will assist you in determining the availability of reference material on your topic:

> *Guide to Reference Books*
> *Walford's Guide to Reference Material*

- Periodical indexes and abstracts are essential tools because they enable you to locate articles in thousands of popular magazines and scholarly journals. The basic difference between abstracts and indexes is that the former not only provide citations for the articles but also summarize the subject matter. The following are just a few that are useful for humanities and social science research:

> *Humanities Index*
> *Abstracts of Native Studies*
> *Sociological Abstracts*

Periodical indexes can be either specific, such as the *Music Index,* or general, such as the *Social Sciences Index.* Some indexes start at the beginning of the century, while others are recent. It is even possible to delve into journals and magazines in the nineteenth century by using *Poole's Index to Periodical Literature* or *Wellesley's Index to Victorian Periodicals.*

Thousands of magazines and journals are published around the world each year. It is possible for you to determine which publications cover your subject area and where a particular journal is indexed by consulting one of the following directories:

> *The Serials Directory*
> *Standard Periodical Directory*
> *Magazines for Libraries*
> *Ulrich's International Periodicals Directory*

These directories include more than just periodicals: they also list newsletters, government publications, year-books, and conference proceedings. "Periodicals" refer to popular magazines and scholarly journals, whereas "Serials" is a broader category that covers periodicals as well as annual reports, yearbooks, newsletters, newspapers, and the proceedings of organizations.

- Citation indexes stand in a class of their own. Even though they can be used for a subject search, they really enable the researcher to identify who has been cited by a given author by providing lists of cited references. *The Arts and Humanities Citation Index* and *The Social Sciences Citation Index* are two major citation indexes.

- Bibliographies are publications listing books, articles, and other sources on specific topics. They are especially useful because someone else has done the searching for you. Once published, however, they become dated. On the other hand, many bibliographies are published annually.

  Annual Bibliography of Victorian Studies
  Bibliographia Canadiana
  International Geographical Bibliography

  The Bibliographic Index is a subject list of bibliographies published separately or as part of books and articles.

- Book reviews may enable you to determine the reliability of a book, and they will often provide additional information and insights on your subject.

  Book Review Digest
  Book Review Index
  Index to Book Reviews in the Humanities

  Many periodical and newspaper indexes also have sections on book reviews.

- Newspapers are a valuable source of information. The following are a sample of many newspaper indexes that will give you quick access to articles and editorials:

  Canadian NewsDisc
  New York Times Index

  If you need lists of newspapers and indexes, consult the following:

  Checklist of Indexes to Canadian Newspapers
  Gale Directory of Publications and Broadcast Media
  Newspapers: A Reference Guide

- A number of publications provide annual reviews of developments in their disciplines or commentaries on publications published during the year.

  Annual Review of Energy
  Film Review Annual

- Biographical indexes are indispensable if you are studying an individual.

    Biography and Genealogy Master Index
    Biography Index

- Masters theses and doctoral dissertations are useful for both content details as well as source information in their bibliographies.

    Canadian Theses
    Dissertation Abstracts Ondisc
    Index to Theses with Abstracts (U.K.)

- There are a number of publications that focus on current affairs. The back issues provide detailed digests of world news and public opinion over the past seventy-five years.

    Editorials on File
    Facts on File

- Some publications, such as the following, outline research aids and important works in specific subjects.

    Sources of Information for Historical Research
    Research Guide to Musicology

- Many speeches, lectures, and papers are delivered each year at conferences and conventions. Transcripts are usually available through indexes, such as the following:

    Bibliographic Guide to Conference Publications
    Directory of Published Proceedings

- Much information is stored on microfiche and microfilm today for preservation purposes and in order to save space. Material in microform includes out-of-print books, government documents, newspapers, periodicals, dissertations, and pamphlets. Microforms in the library are accessible through the library catalogue. There are also guides to microform material, such as the following:

    Microform Research Collections: A Guide
    Subject Guide to Microforms in Print

- If you do not read other languages, you can still gain access to other cultures and perspectives by using the following guides to works in translation:

    Index Translationum
    Translations Register-Index

- There is a wide range of non-print material available in the form of maps, statistics, photographs, taped interviews, films, television, radio, and computer programs. The following are just a few of numerous databases, indexes, and catalogues:

   A-V Online
   Bowker's Complete Video Directory
   Watmedia Database
   Map Link Academic Section
   Statistical Masterfile
   The Media Review Digest

   Many libraries have special audio-visual rooms with catalogues and equipment. Holdings may include films, slides, filmstrips, records, compact discs, laser discs, and video and audio cassettes. Some libraries even permit loans. Many libraries also have special map and atlas collections.

- The current interest in oral history has resulted in many libraries and archives developing collections of audio-taped material. Refer to guides such as *Oral History Collections and Oral History: A Reference Guide and Annotated Bibliography* to determine the accessibility of oral material pertinent to your project. *Words On Cassette* is an extensive bibliography of material on audio-cassette. Consider interviewing and taping experts in your field or approaching eyewitnesses, such as war veterans.

- Professors, teachers, and librarians with special interests can provide useful leads. You can also contact experts by e-mail or raise questions through discussion groups or listservs on the Internet.

- Your library will not contain all existing publications, but an inter-library loan system allows you to obtain material from other libraries. Electronic networks enable libraries to determine the location of a specific source quickly. Copies of journal articles can be obtained through a document delivery service. Approach your librarian if you wish to use these services.

- Compile a list of museums, libraries, art galleries, historical societies, and archives in your community.

2. Sources

The sources that you use to prepare your essay and from which you draw the information and ideas needed to develop your arguments will comprise one or more of three different types: primary, secondary, and tertiary.

Primary sources are original records and data, and include personal memoirs, literary works, the accounts of eyewitnesses, and official documents. Primary material may be in published form, such as an autobiography, a journalist's report, or a government document, such as an international treaty. Primary information is often unpublished, such as letters, diaries, and taped interviews. Much primary material is in non-print form, such as customs, traditions, legends, folklore, music, and song. Inscriptions on old buildings and archaeological artifacts constitute primary material. Primary sources also include original films, photographs, and works of art, as well as statistical data, such as election results and population changes. You can even collect your own primary material by interviewing eyewitnesses, conducting surveys, or by undertaking fieldwork.

A major problem facing researchers when handling primary material is the authenticity of their sources and the reliability of the information. Does a diarist have concealed motives? How trustworthy is the autobiography of a prominent person? Is the reporting of a journalist biased? How accurate are the statistics? How selective is the editing of a documentary film? What is fact and what is fiction?

Verifying (determining authenticity) and **evaluating (determining reliability)** are important facets of research and writing. Most students will not have the time nor the expertise to verify unpublished primary sources, such as determining the authenticity of a medieval manuscript. The issue of authenticity is less of a problem with published primary material, such as the published correspondence of a politician. If you have concerns about the authenticity of a source it may be necessary to consult instructors, librarians, or archivists.

Secondary sources are based on primary material. They are written at a later date than the primary sources on which they are based and from which they draw their conclusions. Secondary sources present another person's evaluation or interpretation of the primary material, and they often develop an argument or point of view. Most of your secondary sources will probably be in the form of books and articles and, increasingly, in electronic documents. Authenticity of secondary sources is seldom a problem, but the credibility and reliability of the material or the views expressed may be questionable.

Questions such as the following will help you determine the reliability of your secondary sources:

• How well known is the author?

• How reputable is the publishing company?

• Is the article published in a respected journal?

• How recently was it published?

• How frequently is the author cited in other sources?

• Is the source based on primary material or just on secondary sources?

• Is the source based on circumstantial evidence or on unfounded assumptions?

• Can important information be confirmed by another source?

• Are the interpretations and arguments well-supported and appropriately documented?

• Does the author use "loaded" language?

• Is the tone and style both formal and correct?

• Has a book been positively reviewed in a journal or newspaper?

Tertiary sources are works that summarize primary and secondary material and provide broad overviews of the information, such as encyclopedias and textbooks. Tertiary sources are especially useful for the preliminary and preparatory reading, but they have limited value as material for the detailed research.

Electronic, or digital, sources can be divided into two main groups: online material available through the Internet and portable databases, such as CD-ROMs, which may be shared via a network. CD-ROMs are not usually as current as online databases, but they can be consulted at no cost in many libraries. Both CD-ROMs and online sources may include primary, secondary, and tertiary material and they are available in formats as varied as text, video, sound, and graphics. Many electronic sources are identical to print versions, while others are only available in digital form, such as online journals and magazines known as e-zines.

Sources in digital form offer many advantages, such as:

- Easy storage of large volumes of information.
- Quick access and retrieval of information.
- Enhancing print versions of documents by adding sound and images.

Online sources have distinct advantages, such as current information and hyperlinks that connect to related web documents. Another advantage is the variety of material and activities available on the Internet.

- You can access primary material in museums, galleries, and archives.
- You can search library catalogues and databases around the world.
- You can discuss problems with other students and even with experts.

The proliferation of online sources and their ease of access has produced a superabundance of information — much of questionable quality. While there are many excellent resources, there are also many dubious databases and web sites. Unlike a printed source, such as a book, which is expensive to publish, an online document can be "published" with relative ease and minimal expense. Furthermore, there is no quality control on the Internet. Online resources are not carefully selected by librarians, as are resources in a library. Therefore, it is especially important to determine the quality of your online sources and to establish their authenticity and reliability.

Many of the criteria used for evaluating traditional primary and secondary sources can be applied to online sources.

Use the criteria and questions listed earlier with the suggestions below to judge your online material. You will also find useful advice on assessing Internet sources by searching online under "evaluating sources." Remember that using information in a discriminating and critical way makes you a more **credible and respected writer.**

- Can you find information that the author is reputable?
- Can you find other documents written by the author?
- Is the document published by a recognized institution?
- How recently was the document published or revised?
- What audience is the document addressing?
- On what type of site is the document published?
- What is the purpose of the document?
- How accurate is the information and can it be verified?
- What is the point of view of the author?
- Are there signs of bias in the document?
- Are there links to other reputable sources?
- Is there a bibliography of reliable sources?

Examine your online material thoroughly and filter the information with caution. Be vigilant: question and think continuously as you read and research. Mindlessly downloading undigested data from the Internet and then pasting it into essay format does not constitute critical thinking. **The computer is simply a tool** and its effectiveness as a tool is determined by how you use it.

Ensure that your Working Bibliography includes a wide range of sources encompassing both the latest online information and traditional sources that reflect primary, secondary, and tertiary material. Evaluate all your sources carefully for **authenticity and reliability.** The evidence that you unearth in your research will fall into two broad categories:

- Factual information or data.
- Ideas, judgments, inferences, theories, and opinions of other writers and scholars.

Part of your task as a researcher is to determine whether a piece of evidence is established fact or personal opinion.

3. The Working Outline

Some students prefer to structure an outline **during the preparatory reading** and to use it as the framework for recording their information. It is often possible to establish a tentative structure in advance, especially in response to "why" questions. Keep the question or purpose uppermost in your mind as you read. Jot down the possible factors around which you might structure an answer to your research question. For example, consider our question "Why did the League of Nations fail to maintain international stability in the 1930s?" As we worked our way through the preparatory reading, we would be looking for possible reasons **why** the League failed to maintain international stability in the 1930s. List these reasons on a separate page headed Working Outline, as shown below.

Working Outline

A. *Introduction*
B. I   *Structure of League*
     II   *U.S. not a member*
     III *Shortcomings of Covenant*
     IV   *Motives of member states*
     V   *Failure to resolve crises*
C. *Conclusion*

List as many factors or sections as you can in the body of your Working Outline, but remember that they must be linked to the purpose of your essay. **The research question shapes the contents of your Working Outline**. There is no special order and no magic number of sections in a Working Outline. List as many as you can and then consolidate and reduce them if there are too many. From three to six sections should handle most questions comfortably.

You are researching and developing a response to your question — you are not simply writing a narrative chronicle, a descriptive account, or a biographical report. Ensure that your Working Outline does not lead you in the direction of one of the above approaches. Chronological outlines, for example, can easily lead to narrative chronicles.

A Working Outline is not a straightjacket that inhibits creativity, because it is not a final plan for the essay. It is only a provisional structure to promote the clustering and classification of ideas, insights, and information. The **Working Outline is flexible** — you may add sections during the research or you may delete some. Although developing a tentative structure will take more time initially, the time will be regained later because the outlining and drafting will be quicker. Furthermore, since the sections of the Working Outline are a direct response to the research question, they represent an emerging thesis or argument. However, a more immediate advantage of a Working Outline is having a framework for recording ideas and information.

The Working Outline can be used with either notepaper, index cards, or a computer to record information. Read carefully the research procedures described on pages 17–28 because they contain many suggestions on notetaking not repeated here. If you prefer notepaper for your research, allocate a separate page to each section of the Working Outline opposite and write in the section heading at the top of the page, as shown below.

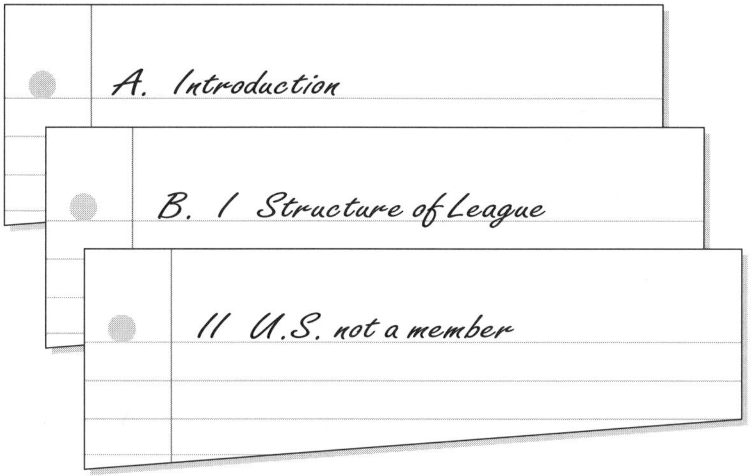

A. Introduction

B. 1 Structure of League

II U.S. not a member

Analysis is the detailed examination and dissection of your material in accordance with the question or purpose of your essay.   Besides guiding the analysis, the research question also shapes the structure of the Working Outline, as explained on the previous two pages. Therefore, the sections of the Working Outline provide the analytical framework for the research by supplying a structure for classifying and recording the relevant ideas and information.

Read through your first source, for example the Northedge book coded LNLT, as explained on pages 10 and 11, looking specifically for information relevant to your question.   On page 51 there is reference to the ease with which states could join and leave the League.   Since the problem of membership concerns the structure of the organization and "Structure of the League" is B.I on your Working Outline, write the note under B.I as shown below.   Indicate the source code and page number in the left margin.

	B. I Structure of League
LNLT 51	Only minimum qualifications needed to join the League. Could leave as easily as they joined.

Reflect on what you have done:
  • You have discovered relevant information pertaining to the research question.
  • You have recorded it in note form under the appropriate section of the Working Outline.
  • You have indicated the source code and page number.

Continue reading through all your sources searching for information and ideas relevant to your question, and then systematically record your notes under the appropriate sections of the Working Outline, adding the source code and page reference as explained.   When one section is full, head another page and continue recording your notes.   You can use both sides of the notepaper for this method.

If you prefer index cards for your research, reread pages 23–27 carefully because the two methods are similar. The only difference is that if you have pre-structured a Working Outline you can assign a section number to each card, as shown in the right-hand corner of the example below. In this example the note refers to the ease with which states could join and leave the League. Since the problem of membership concerns the structure of the organization and "Structure of the League" is B.I on your Working Outline, assign a number I, as shown. The source code and page number are entered, as explained earlier.

LNLT 51   */*

Only minimum qualifications needed to join the League. Could leave as easily as they joined.

If you are using index cards **with a Working Outline** each card will contain **three** items, as shown above:

1. Source code and page   2. Note   3. Section number.

If you prefer to use a computer, you can use index card software and set up electronic cards and enter the details as shown above. Or, you can use a word processor to create separate pages of electronic notepaper (or files) for each section of the Working Outline. You can then record the information in the appropriate file, as explained on page 120.

Sometimes a piece of information will not fit under one of the sections. You will either have to create another section in your Working Outline to incorporate the information, or you will have to discard the information as irrelevant to the essay. **Do not create a Miscellaneous or General section** because it will become a repository for inconsequential odds and ends and will soon dominate the other sections.

Once you have completed the research, your notes (on index cards, notepaper, or computer) will be grouped according to the sections of the Working Outline. It is impossible to write a final copy straight from these notes. A number of intermediate stages are necessary to ensure quality. The first stage is primarily a name change. Once the research is finished, the Working Outline becomes the Basic Outline, as shown below. Some of your sections may have changed during the course of the research. You will notice in our example that we have eliminated B.II "US not a Member" and B.III "Shortcomings of Covenant" because each section contained insufficient information. These changes necessitated altering the numbering of the sections of the Basic Outline, as shown below. The basic structure is now in place, though there may be a change in the order of the sections during the outlining and drafting.

Working Outline

A. Introduction
B. I   Structure of League
    II   U.S. not a member
    III   Shortcomings of Covenant
    IV   Motives of member states
    V   Failure to resolve crises
C. Conclusion

Basic Outline

A. Introduction
B. I   Structure of League
    II   Motives of member states
    III   Failure to resolve crises
C. Conclusion

Continue with the Skeleton Outline and the rest of the outlining and drafting, as explained on pages 33–53.

4. Illustrations

There are two major types of illustrations: tables and figures. **Tables** contain statistical data, while **figures** consist of photographs, maps, drawings, graphs, diagrams, charts, and pictures. Software, such as spreadsheets or graphics programs, allows you to do most illustrations on a computer. Computers also allow you to scan information and to merge and embed illustrations in the text. If computer facilities are not available, tables and figures can still be prepared by hand. Aim for clarity and simplicity when laying out your illustrations. Demonstrated on the following pages are some of the more commonly used illustrations.

Tables

Table 1. Population of Metropolitan Areas, Selected Years.			
CITY	1988	1992	1996
		(thousands)	
Toronto	3,813,2	4,116,9	4,444,7
Montreal	3,112,3	3,251,1	3,359,0
Vancouver	1,524,9	1,690,8	1,891,4
Ottawa-Hull	884,0	974,6	1,030,5
Edmonton	808,7	870,7	891,5
Quebec	633,6	672,3	697,6
Winnipeg	651,9	667,9	676,7
Halifax	312,1	331,4	346,8
Regina	195,2	196,1	199,2
St. John's	167,8	177,4	177,8
Saint John	125,6	129,4	129,1

Source: *Canada Year Book 1999* (Ottawa: Statistics Canada, 1998), 94.

Figures

Maps

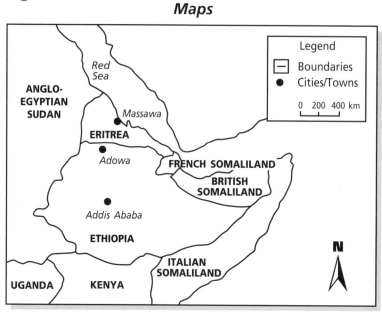

Fig. 1. Ethiopia's Borders, 1935.

Organizational Charts

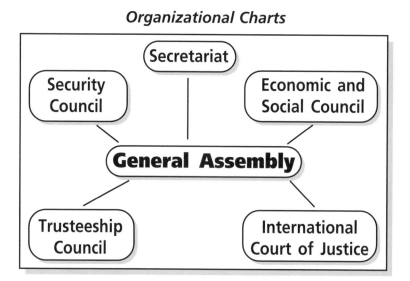

Fig. 2. The United Nations System.

Line Graphs

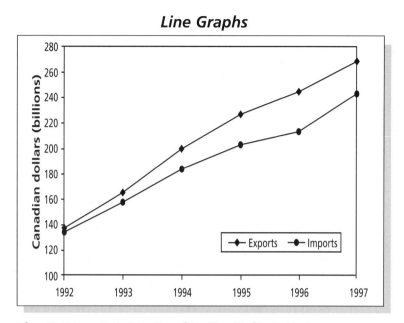

Fig. 3. Canada's Trade with the United States.
Source: Balance of International Payments, 4th Quarter 1997, Statistics Canada.

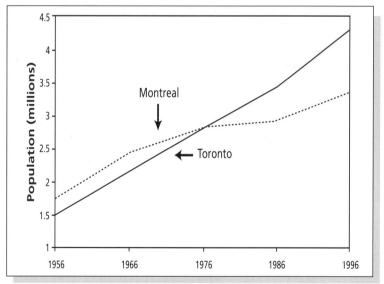

Fig. 4. Population Comparison of Toronto and Montreal.
Source: John R. Colombo, ed., *The Canadian Global Almanac* (Toronto: Macmillan, 1998), 54.

Bar/Column Charts

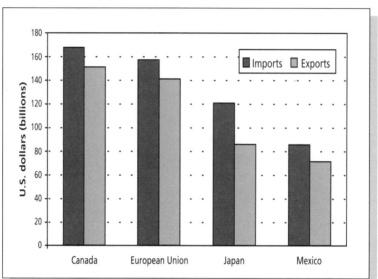

Fig. 5. United States' Main Trading Partners, 1997.
Source: U.S. Department of Commerce, Bureau of the Census.

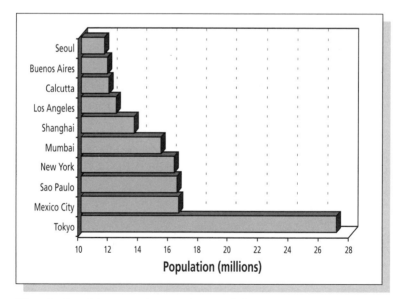

Fig. 6. World's Most Populous Cities, 1997.
Source: *The World Almanac and Book of Facts* (Mahwah, NJ: K-111 Reference Corp., 1997), 838.

Circle/Pie Charts

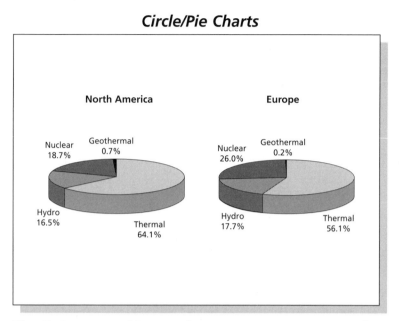

Fig. 7. Sources of Energy in Europe and North America.
Source: *1995 Energy Statistics Yearbook* (New York: United
Nations, 1997), 432 and 448.

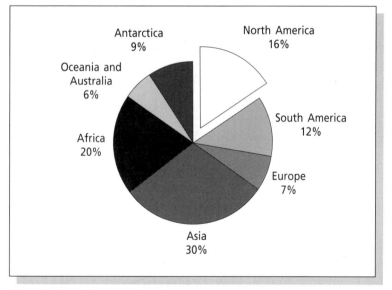

Fig. 8. Continents by Area.
Source: *The World Almanac and Book Of Facts* (Mahwah,
NJ: K-111 Reference Corp., 1997), 838.

Climate Graphs

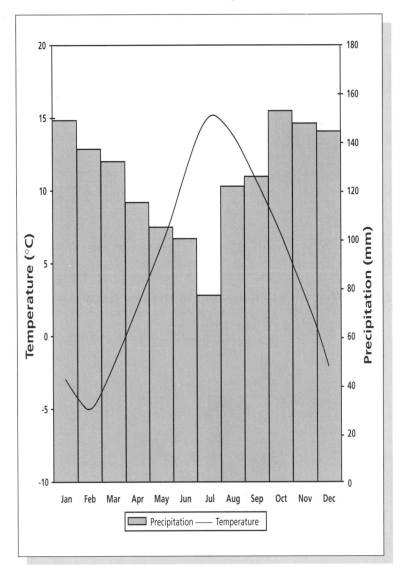

Fig. 9. Climate of St. John's, 1942-1990.
Source: *Canadian Climate Normals 1961-1990*, Environment Canada, April 1993.

5. The Abstract

An abstract forces the writer to examine closely the organization, argument, and presentation of the essay. It can also enhance the overall impression that your paper creates. It is written in concise essay form of between 100 and 300 words, and placed on the page immediately following the title page. Short abstracts of about 100 words are sometimes placed on the title page. Ask your instructor whether an abstract is required and, if so, what the specific requirements are and where it should be placed. The abstract is a short synopsis of the essay and, therefore, it must be written last. It must not be confused with the introduction, with which there might, however, be some overlap. The abstract may include all or some of the following features:

- Discussion of the topic and the selection of a specific problem or issue and its importance as a field for investigation.

- A clear statement of the essay's purpose or the research question.

- A statement of the thesis or argument and an explanation of the structure for the development of the thesis/argument.

- The conclusions reached.

- A definition of the limits of the assignment; a clarification of what is and is not being considered.

- A discussion of the various sources, primary and secondary, and their usefulness, as well as the research aids, libraries, and archives used.

- The documentation system and the nature of the list of sources, such as an annotated bibliography, for example, and whether explanatory footnotes or endnotes have been used.

- A list of the contents of the appendix.

The question you should ask yourself is this: If the essay is lost and only the abstract survives, will it convey to the reader a clear picture of the essay, its central argument, and its organization?

6. Seminars

The seminar is an organized discussion focused around the presentation of an argument or point of view by the leader. It is not a debate but a **collaborative forum** for the exploration, examination, and exchange of ideas and opinions and an attempt to resolve problems arising out of the presentation. The seminar format works well with groups of ten to fifteen students. Participants are seated in a circle, oval, or horseshoe formation which promotes face to face discussion. The leader presents and substantiates a point of view on an important issue followed by a guided discussion. The leader concludes the seminar by summing up the discussion.

The preparation for presenting a seminar is identical to the process for preparing a research paper. The instructor may assign the **topic** or you may be free to select your own topic. **Narrowing** the topic to a specific issue or problem is especially important in a seminar because usually you will have limited time to present your point of view. Superficial presentations lacking a clearly defined focus inevitably generate rambling discussions. The next step is to build a wide-ranging **working bibliography** relevant to the issue or problem on which you have focused. While you are building your working bibliography remember to jot down potential questions that can serve to help you identify more readily the purpose or objective of the presentation. Like a major paper, the **research question** provides direction for the seminar. Next spend some time on background reading, keeping the research question uppermost in your mind. This **preparatory reading** is an essential part of the base of the iceberg — your presentation is the one tenth above the water.

Armed with a thorough understanding of the focus of your seminar, a substantial list of sources, and an incisive question, you are ready to assemble your material and start analyzing and recording the relevant ideas and information. An **organized collection of notes** is as essential for a seminar as it is for a research paper. The pathway you forged while preparing research papers is similar for preparing seminars. The advantage of a well travelled pathway is that it can be easily modified for use in a wide variety of assignments.

Once you have completed analyzing and recording the relevant information and ideas, you can start **shaping and composing** your answer to the research question. Like an essay, your answer represents your thesis, argument, or point of view — it is the glue that will hold the seminar together. And like an essay, the clarity of your presentation will be determined largely by its **structure and style**. The Point-form Outline will provide the structure, while style is the manner of your delivery. Whether you are writing an essay or presenting a seminar, the objective is identical — communicating your message clearly.

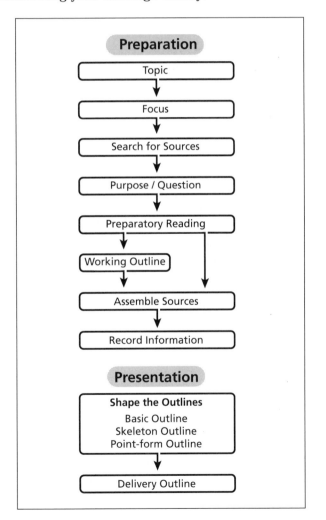

Structure your Basic, Skeleton, and Point-form outlines in exactly the same way that you shaped your research papers. Although a seminar is the oral equivalent of an essay, **do not write or type a rough copy.** You may be tempted to read from the written script or memorize it and thereby lose some of the spontaneity necessary to maintain good contact with your audience. A Point-form Outline based on extensive research and careful thought will enable you to communicate your thesis **clearly and succinctly.** Be realistic, however, about the amount of detail you include in your outline because you may have limited time to present it and your audience has limits on how much they can absorb.

Some students prefer to write their points on index (or cue) cards when delivering their presentations. However, audiences can get irritated by speakers flipping through their cards. Furthermore, you could panic if you drop a card or they get out of order. An alternative method is to reduce your Point-form Outline to key words and write the abbreviated outline on a page of notepaper (or on a firm piece of white cardboard). Having the overall structure and the supporting details mapped out in front of you will facilitate your presentation and will allow you to refer quickly to a point if you get flustered. Circle the main sections and highlight the subsections for quick and easy reference. You can also jot down suggestions for delivery in the margin, such as where to pause or where to repeat important information.

Rehearsing is essential for successful seminar presentations. You may wish to tape-record your presentation and then play it back to detect flaws. Rehearsing in front of a mirror is another option. You could also arrange for some friends to act as an audience and comment on your presentation. A video recording will allow you to review your delivery and fine tune your non-verbal language, often called "body language." Careful preparation and rehearsing will not only improve your presentation, it will also build your sense of confidence.

What props and equipment should you use to supplement your presentation? Generally, instructors suggest that students minimize the use of audio-visual aids in seminar presentations. Partly this is because multimedia equipment can be distracting in smaller formal and scholarly settings.

Instructors also want students to master the skills of verbal communication instead of allowing technology to become the focus of the presentation. There is also the possibility of high tech equipment malfunctioning and creating anxiety for the speaker. Check with your instructor well in advance of the seminar about what equipment is permitted.

Seminar leaders should prepare a handout and distribute it to the participants a week in advance of the meeting. Suggested items for the handout include the following:

- Title
- Purpose/Research question
- Thesis/Argument/Point of view
- Outline of major sections
- Text readings
- Additional readings
- Issues and questions for discussion

Communicating a **well-supported point of view** to the group is your prime responsibility. Like writing style in an essay, the manner of your delivery will enhance the impact of your message. The following suggestions will help improve the delivery of your presentation:

- Use precise, formal language
- Choose your words carefully
- Articulate clearly and fluently
- Vary the volume and tone of your voice
- Vary the pace of your delivery
- Maintain eye contact with your audience
- Stand (or sit) erect
- Pause occasionally for emphasis
- Use humour sparingly
- Be enthusiastic
- Breathe naturally
- Dress appropriately
- Avoid excessive hand gestures
- Conclude with confidence

Once the presentation is completed, the leader guides the ensuing discussion. First, deal with questions requiring clarification of points raised in the presentation and then move on to an exploration of the thesis and related issues. Group members will already have pondered the list of issues and questions handed out in advance of the seminar.

A well-presented seminar invariably generates an animated and stimulating discussion. Some discussions become heated and passionate and need "cooling," others become sluggish and need a stimulus in the form of further questions or a provocative comment from the leader. Do not distribute any material during the seminar lest it divert the attention of the participants from listening to your presentation and engaging in the subsequent discussion.

Do not dominate the discussion. Remaining in the background as leader will shift responsibility to the members for sustaining the discussion and will also allow you to listen and make brief notes. These notes can be used to compose a summary to conclude the seminar. It is a demanding, but rewarding task to conduct a discussion that is both interactive and free-flowing, yet focused and formal — especially immediately following your presentation. Like all skills, your performance will improve with practice. Public speaking and leading discussion groups are valuable skills to acquire.

Preparation is not only important for presenters but for participants as well. Make detailed notes and list questions and comments as you study the assigned readings. Listen attentively to the leader's presentation and add to your notes. **Active listening,** both during the presentation and the discussion, requires focused concentration, an openness to other points of view, a skeptical attitude, and the listing of incisive questions and reasoned responses.

Continue to listen carefully to the perspectives of others during the discussion following the presentation. Jot down further questions and ideas in your notes. **Listen to understand,** not simply to respond critically to other participants. Pose questions, raise interesting insights, and respond to comments at appropriate opportunities. Always be respectful of the opinions of others and do not interrupt another participant. At all costs **avoid attempting to monopolize** a seminar discussion.

The seminar leaders will be evaluated for how effectively they have presented their point of view and also how well they have led the discussion. The participants are often evaluated on the basis of their contributions to the discussion. Traditionally, the term "participation" has been used to designate the level of input by participants. However, the use of the term encourages some students to "sound off" because excessive talking, often empty, is assumed to represent "participation." Instructors look for involvement in the form of **active listening, incisive questioning, sensitive engagement, insightful comments, open-minded attitudes, and enthusiastic participation.** Terms like "engagement," "commitment," and "contribution" are more commonly used today to assess the roles of seminar participants.

Active participation in a seminar can be a stimulating learning experience, but like all learning it is governed by that iron law which declares that what you get out is directly proportional to what you put in — whether you are the presenter or a participant.

❖ ❖ ❖

Another version of the seminar, sometimes called a "research seminar," can be used in smaller groups of five or six students. This type of seminar takes place at the draft stage of the process of writing an essay.

- Leader/writer distributes draft copies of the essay to the participants one week before the seminar.

- Participants submit written comments and suggestions to the leader one day before the seminar.

- Leader reads the comments and prepares responses.

- Leader starts the seminar by responding to the comments and suggestions.

- Leader chairs the ensuing discussion on issues pertaining to the essay.

- Leader/writer revises and fine tunes the draft and submits the final essay one week later.

7.   Examinations

Introduction

Instructors frequently use the essay format when setting examinations, whether they are take-home examinations or examinations written under supervision. Essay-style examinations can measure a wide range of skills, including:

- Addressing and interpreting a question
- Developing and substantiating an argument
- The logical organization of ideas
- Clear, precise expression
- Critical judgment
- Thinking clearly under time constraints

These skills cannot be demonstrated in a knowledge vacuum: a sound grasp of the basic course material and the theoretical framework is essential. **Knowledge and skills are inseparable in the writing of good essay answers.** There are many similarities between the major and minor term essays and the examination essay, though the scale may be different. The best practice for writing successful essay examinations is to develop and refine your thinking and writing skills during the course of the academic year — and the best preparation for an examination starts on the first day of the course.

Discuss with your instructor well before the examination:

- What will be covered and what will not be covered in the examination.
- The precise meaning of common examination terms.
- What criteria will be used in assessing the answers.
- Whether the questions have to be answered in the order in which they appear on the examination paper.
- Whether you should double-space or single-space your writing.

- Any other matters, such as the use of the first person pronoun.

Read the entire examination paper slowly.

- Pay careful attention to all the instructions. For example, confusing compulsory and optional questions could be disastrous.

- Read the questions carefully, underlining keywords, such as "analyze" and "discuss."

- Think carefully before selecting your questions (if a choice is permitted).

Consider the following before you start writing:

- Map out a schedule for answering the questions by allocating your time according to the marks awarded for each question. Allow time at the end for proofreading.

- If you are permitted to answer questions in any order, do those that you know best first.

- Do not waste your time writing out the questions; just number your answers correctly.

Approach each question carefully.

- Determine the precise meaning of keywords, such as "discuss" and "analyze." Misinterpreting important terms could create problems.

- Address the question exactly as it is phrased. Do not sidestep the question or substitute a title of your own creation.

- Never change a question to suit a prepared answer.

- Think carefully before tackling each question. Attempt a fresh interpretation.

- **Plan your answers.** Brainstorm the question and jot down relevant ideas and information. Then arrange a Basic Outline using the ABC formula, followed by a brief Skeleton Outline with supporting details, before you start.

- **Never** write a rough draft and then a good copy. Use your time more profitably. You can ensure neatness, organization, and accuracy by thoughtful planning and careful proofreading.

Reflect on the structure of the answer.

- Keep the introduction short. Brief background information and a clear thesis statement (response to the question) is all that is needed for an examination introduction. Some instructors prefer just a statement of the thesis and no background information.

- Develop and substantiate your thesis/argument/answer/ point of view in the body.

- Complete your answer with a brief concluding paragraph in which you draw together the main threads of your answer and drive home your argument.

- Use your Basic Outline for each answer as a formula for shaping the paragraph structure. Avoid subheadings.

- Write in a clear and formal style. Precise, articulate expression has persuasive power.

The body is the most important part of an examination answer.

- You have limited time, so you must select just the essential and relevant information needed to support your answer.

- Focus on your thesis and ensure that all the information is linked explicitly to it. Simply pouring out all you know on a topic will destroy the clarity of your answer.

- Convincing interpretations, judgments, and arguments have to be anchored in solid evidence and concrete examples.

- Give your answers depth and detail and avoid vague generalities.

- Ensure that there is a logical sequence to the development of your ideas.

- Avoid speculating and conjecturing about hypothetical situations. "What if . . ." has no place in an answer.

- Do not try to force memorized quotations into your answers. If, however, you have remembered lines relevant to your answer, then by all means use them.

Remember that examiners reward thoughtful, lucid essays.

- Developing a clear and convincing response to each question is your sole task. The clarity of your answer is shaped largely by its structure and style.

- Examiners are looking for incisive analysis and argument, not for summaries of texts and superficial surveys.

- Remember the cliché: quality, not quantity. It is true.

- **Write legibly.** A paper that is easy to read will have a positive impact on the examiner. Avoid using correcting fluid and asterisks and arrows to make changes and additions.

- Number your pages accurately.

Watch the clock.

- Follow the time schedule you mapped out at the beginning of the examination.

- Allow time at the end to proofread your answers. Remember that proofreading is fine-tuning, not major revising.

- Complete the paper. Do not leave a scribbled list of points at the end with an apology to the examiner that you ran out of time. **Completing an examination within the time limit is part of the test.**

Do not panic if you are confronted by a difficult paper. Scour the depths of your memory for all relevant information and plan an outline. You can probably squeeze through in a crisis with a moderate amount of knowledge, good organization, and polished writing skills. Any attempt is better than no attempt at all.

Essays

Supervised examinations containing essay-style questions can take different forms:

- open-book
- notes permitted
- no notes permitted
- the question assigned in advance by the teacher
- design your own question and prepare your response in advance
- no advance knowledge of the question

Let us assume that you are writing your final examination in a history course, and the questions have not been set in advance. After carefully considering the list of questions, you select the following one: "How did external factors influence the confederation of the British North American colonies in 1867?" The question is worth fifty marks out of a total of 100 marks. Since the examination is two hours in length, you allow yourself one hour to plan and write the answer.

First, spend a few minutes brainstorming the question and jotting down relevant ideas and information to help you plan your response. Arrange your main points in a Basic Outline, and then create a Skeleton Outline containing the supporting details. As we demonstrated earlier in this manual, the outlines provide a formula for developing your paragraphs. In a shorter examination answer, the Basic Outline establishes the paragraph structure, while the Skeleton Outline supplies the supporting details, as demonstrated on the following pages.

Once the structure is mapped out with the supporting details, it is a relatively easy task to write the essay. Remember to follow the advice spelled out on the previous four pages when writing your examination essay answers. Sample outlines and a response to the question are shown on the pages ahead. You will notice that the response follows the structure and details in the outlines.

Basic Outline

A. Introduction

B. I.   British Influence
    II. American Civil War
    III. Economic incentives
    IV. Military threat

C. Conclusion

Skeleton Outline

A. Introduction
    – Historical context
    – Thesis statement

B. I. British influence
       1. Favoured union
       2. Role in the Maritimes
       3. Financial incentive

    II. American Civil War
        1. Possibility of American attack
        2. Fear of annexation

    III. Economic incentives
         1. Abrogation of Reciprocity Treaty
         2. Economic setback
         3. Economic union appealing

    IV. Military threat
        1. Fenian raids
        2. Quest for Security

C. Conclusion

The creation of the "Great Coalition" in 1864 was a clear indication that Canadian politicians anxiously desired a practical solution to the persistent problems of political instability and deadlock that had plagued Canadian politics since the 1840s. Discussions, already underway for a union of the Maritime colonies, provided a further stimulus for the creation of a united British North America. Although internal initiatives shaped the advent of Confederation in 1867, external factors were the driving force that brought about the union of British North America.

Britain played a crucial role in promoting the idea of a British North American union. British officials had long favoured a less dependent status for the colonies because they found the cost of their defence increasingly burdensome. Consequently, the Colonial Office sought to accelerate the process of separation and independence by intervening directly in Maritime affairs in 1865 to curb the popularity of the faction opposed to confederation. In New Brunswick, Britain ordered Governor Gordon, a long time opponent of confederation, to reverse his stance and encourage the movement towards union. In Nova Scotia, Britain replaced the governor with someone more sympathetic to the union cause. In addition to this political manoeuvering, Britain also promised to help finance the proposed Intercolonial Railway to encourage commercial cooperation among the colonies.

While Britain worked hard to encourage the movement towards amalgamation, another external factor — the American Civil War — provided a major impetus for British North American union. British North Americans became increasingly uneasy with the war raging on their doorstep. As Anglo-American tensions mounted, many feared the prospect of Northern retribution against the British colonies. Fears of American annexation swept through the colonies as many contemplated the possibility that the victorious Northern forces might seek retaliation against those colonies that had supported the South during the conflict. The speeches of several American politicians explicitly advocating annexation and warning of retribution heightened these fears. Colonial politicians believed that a British North American union would be an effective way to fend off American annexation initially, and in later years, thwart American expansion northwards.

External economic pressures also furthered the notion of a federation of British North America. The introduction of free trade in Britain from the mid 19th century and the subsequent loss of protected markets for British North American products forced the colonies to seek alternative outlets. Actively encouraged by the British government, they sought a commercial agreement with their southern neighbours and in 1854 Lord Elgin signed the Reciprocity Treaty. It was a far-reaching free trade agreement covering a period of ten years. The treaty expired in 1865 and British North Americans, who had benefited significantly from this agreement, waited anxiously to see whether the Americans would renew it. But the American Senate decide to terminate the treaty. The abrogation of the treaty marked a major setback for British North Americans as it had been of substantial commercial, as well as psychological, value. The loss of a prominent trading partner forced British North Americans to consider other means of fostering trade and commerce. The idea of forging a commercial union amongst themselves became increasingly appealing as markets in Britain and the United States continued to shrink.

The Fenian attacks highlighted the military vulnerability of the colonies and furthered the arguments in favour of union. The Fenians were revolutionary republican Irishmen who had devised a grandiose scheme to capture British North America and use it as ransom to negotiate the liberation of Ireland. The Fenians launched several raids from bases in the United States into New Brunswick and Canada West in 1865 and 1866. Although the damage inflicted was minor, the psychological threat generated by the Fenians was far from inconsequential. At a time when the British North American colonies were feeling increasingly insecure, the Fenian menace consolidated sentiments for a union that would create an effective military force and thereby ensure their defence.

The British North American colonies were successfully and peacefully confederated in 1867 with the warm endorsement of the British government. While the impetus for change was initiated from within the colonies, it was powerful external forces emanating from across the Atlantic and from south of the border that finally drove home the necessity for union.

Comparisons

Traditionally, "comparing" has meant focusing on similarities. But today comparing is widely accepted as including similarities and differences. "Contrasting," however, means concentrating on differences only. Comparing and contrasting is more difficult than writing the single-focus essay described in this guide. Comparative questions require that you show the connection or relationship (in the form of similarities and/or differences) between two ideas, individuals, or developments. Comparisons are not descriptive compositions or biographical chronicles. **Comparisons are essays with a thesis or argument**, regardless of whether they are examination answers or major assignments. Descriptive narrative is not comparative analysis.

Let us assume that you have chosen the following comparative question in your final examination: "Compare and/or contrast the federal systems of government in the United States and in Canada." When selecting comparative questions, it is essential that you have a thorough under-standing of **both** aspects or issues to be compared. Since the structure of a comparative essay is more complex than that of a single-focus essay, you must allow more planning time. **Do not start writing your answer until you have planned the structure.** Spend a few minutes brainstorming the major similarities and differences between the two systems of government. Jot down these similarities and differences in separate columns, as shown below.

Similarities	Differences
Federations	Senate
Passing legislation	Cabinet
Entrenched rights	Elections
Supreme Court	Powers
	Head of state
	Head of government
	Legislation
	Parties
	Monarchy/Republic

Once you have identified the major similarities and differences, you have to decide whether the similarities or the differences dominate the relationship. It is also possible that they may be evenly balanced. Determining the extent of the similarities and differences is an important step, because it will **shape both your thesis and the structure of the answer.** In our example, there are more differences than similarities and, therefore, it is logical to focus the answer on the major differences between the federal systems of government in Canada and in the United States.

You cannot cover all the differences (or similarities) in a comparative examination answer because of time constraints. Therefore, you have to be selective when setting up your Basic Outline and focus on only the most important features of the relationship, as shown below.

Basic Outline

A. Introduction

B. I   Monarchy/Republic
    II   Elections
    III Head of government
    IV   Cabinet
    V   Legislation
    VI   Senate

C. Conclusion

Each major feature in the body has to be developed by explicitly linking the two systems of government and then demonstrating the connections with specific examples and details. There must be corresponding examples and details to draw comparisons — **you cannot compare something with nothing**. The next step is to structure the Skeleton Outline showing the supporting details for each section. Once again the outlines will provide a formula for developing the paragraphs, as shown on the next page.

Skeleton Outline

A. *Introduction*   *(paragraph)*
    1. Background
    2. Thesis
B. *I. Monarchy/Republic*   *(paragraph)*
    1. US: combined functions
    2. Can: separated
    3. Unique situations
    II. Elections   *(paragraph)*
    1. US: prescribed pattern (2/4 yrs.)
    2. Can: flexible (within 5 yrs.)
    III. Head of government   *(paragraph)*
    1. Can: p.m. in Commons
    2. US: pres. not in Congress
    3. "Job security"
    IV. Cabinet   *(paragraph)*
    1. US: not in Congress
    2. Can: elected to Commons
    3. Administrative role
    V. Legislation   *(paragraph)*
    1. Quicker in Can
    2. Often deadlocked in US
    3. Consequences of failure
    VI. Senate   *(paragraph)*
    1. US: elected, powerful
    2. Can: appointed, limited powers
C. *Conclusion*   *(paragraph)*

Once the structure is mapped out with the supporting details, it is easy to weave the comparative answer together. State the thesis consisely in the introduction, and ensure that the sections of the body clearly demonstrate the links and the relationships needed to support the thesis. You cannot expect the examiner to establish the connections; **that is your responsibility.** Finally, complete your answer by drawing the comparative threads together in a concluding paragraph. A sample comparative answer is reproduced on the following pages. You will notice that it follows closely the structure and details in the outlines.

Americans designed their constitution — a constitution unique for its many "checks and balances" — following their victory in the 1776 revolutionary war against the British. Canada's system of government developed by way of a slow evolution that resulted in almost all of the features of the British parliamentary system being maintained. Canada and the United States share a continent and increasingly they share similar cultural characteristics, yet Canadian political culture has remained distinctive.

The main distinguishing characteristic of the two systems is that Canada is a constitutional monarchy, whereas the United States is a republic. The U.S. is somewhat unique among republics because it has combined the ceremonial head of state function with the hands-on head of government function: both are embodied in the elected president. In Canada, the head of state is the governor-general who is the representative of the monarch, and the head of government is the prime minister. Since it is the prime minister, as head of the elected government, who chooses the governor-general, it is clear that the real power lies in the hands of the prime minister. Only in unique situations of constitutional turmoil does a governor-general play a decision-making role in the process of government.

Elections in the United States follow a prescribed pattern. There are biennial elections in November, at which time all the seats in the House of Representatives and one third of the Senate seats are up for renewal. The president is elected every four years, in November. Following the more traditional parliamentary model, elections in Canada are only constitutionally mandated to occur within five years of a previous election, and the only representatives elected are the members of the House of Commons. However, depending on political developments, elections can occur at any time during that five year period, and they often do. Canadian elections, therefore, follow a more flexible pattern than the prescribed American electoral procedure.

In the Canadian system, the prime minister is an elected member of Parliament who is usually the leader of the party that controls the most seats in the House of Commons. In the American system, the president is elected by popular vote (except on rare occasions) and then confirmed in office by the Electoral College. However, the president may not sit or vote in either congressional house. The only way to remove an American president during a four year term is by way of impeachment, a process that ultimately requires a two-thirds majority in the Senate. A Canadian prime minister has much less job security and can be forced to resign at any time, following a vote of no-confidence in the House of Commons. It is not unusual for Canada to have more than one prime minister during the four year term of an American president. Attaining the position of head of government and then maintaining it differs substantially in the two countries.

Although the cabinets are appointed by the American president and the Canadian prime minister, they function differently in each country. Like the president, American cabinet members are not permitted to sit in Congress. This means that the American president can appoint anyone he or she wants — not just an elected politician — to a cabinet post. In Canada, on the other hand, cabinet ministers are traditionally selected from the elected members of the House of Commons, and occasionally from the non-elected Senate. If any other selection is made, it is customary that the newly-appointed cabinet minister attempts to win a seat in the House of Commons at an early opportunity. Canadian cabinets are, by their very nature, political, and consequently they play an influential role in shaping public policy and passing laws. The American cabinet members do not have the same influence with regard to shaping legislation; indeed, their main function is the administration of their departments, a task that is largely the responsibility of a non-political deputy minister in Canada.

By concentrating political power in the elected House of Commons, the Canadian system facilitates the quick passage of legislation. The Canadian Senate can stall a bill but ultimately it cannot reject it outright. (The "stalling process" often has the effect of publicizing a bill's defects, and public opinion can then influence the House of Commons to withdraw the bill, or change it significantly.) The governor-general signs into law all bills passed by both houses. Passage of legislation in the United Sates is seldom as efficient a process. The two houses of Congress may be controlled by different parties or the president's party may even be in a minority in both houses. Furthermore, American legislators do not vote along party lines, a breach *of loyalty not permitted in the Canadian parliamentary system. As a result, legislation is often deadlocked for months, as deals of one kind or another are made among various political factions in Congress — deals that often gut the original intent of the legislation. Although the Canadian prime minister and the cabinet have a great deal of power when it comes to initiating and passing legislation — power that an American president can only envy — there is a price to pay: if a major bill fails to pass in the Commons, the prime minister and cabinet have to resign and an election is called. If a bill fails to pass in the American system, the failure cannot be blamed on the president or the cabinet and their jobs are not threatened.*

Other than the name, the two Senates have little in common. In the United States, the Senate is an elected body, and a powerful one; it can initiate or block legislation, and it must approve all foreign treaties. Each state elects two senators to a term of six years. However, since one third of the Senate seats come up for renewal every two years, the composition of the Senate can change significantly within a six year period. Canadian senators are appointed by the prime minister, and they can serve until they reach 75 years of age. In a way, the Canadian Senate is a residual version of the British House of Lords, and like the House of Lords it has limited powers, such as "stalling" legislation. The elected American Senate, representing all the states equally, is a much more powerful body.

Many Canadians want to abolish the appointed Senate or change it to an elected body. But even those Canadians who favour a reformed Senate are reluctant to give it the constitutional powers of the American Senate. Some Canadians even suggest replacing the monarchy, but retaining a separate head of state and head of government. Likewise, some Americans can see the advantage of separating the ceremonial function of government from the governing function, but most still believe in the advantages of the constitutional system created by the founders of the American republic. Although there is an ongoing debate about modifying the present systems of government, differences still dominate the political landscape in North America, and two democratic traditions with deep historical roots continue to co-exist comfortably.

Glossary

Essay-style questions can be phrased in a variety of ways. Some questions may only require the presentation of information, such as "Describe conditions in the Balkans in the spring of 1914." Other questions may require a point of view or argument, such as "How successful was Reconstruction after the American Civil War?" Questions requiring a response to a quotation are also common, such as "Assess the following comment: 'The League of Nations was primarily an organization for preserving the privileges of the major powers.'" The keyword in each question will indicate the type of response required. Consult your instructor about ambiguous terminology such as "analyze" and "discuss" **before the examination**. Listed below are some of the more common terms used in examinations.

Assess: Examine and judge the strengths and weaknesses of an idea or argument and justify your conclusions.

- Assess Paul Kennedy's explanation of the rise and fall of imperial powers.

Analyze: Identify and examine carefully the details and ideas and explain their relationship and/or demonstrate their importance.

- Analyze the factors underlying U.S. foreign policy in the 1930s.

Compare: Show the connection or relationship between different individuals, events, or issues by focusing on the similarities and/or differences.

- Compare the federal systems of government in the United States and Canada.

Contrast: Show the connection or relationship between different individuals, events, or issues by focusing on the differences only.

- Contrast the roles of the Canadian prime minister and the American president.

**Compare/
Contrast:** Sometimes both are used in a question.

- Compare and contrast Canadian and American foreign policies in the Cold War era.

• Compare and/or contrast the successes of the League of Nations and the United Nations.

Criticize: Similar in requirements to Assess. Criticize does not mean focusing solely on weaknesses or negative aspects. "Critical analysis" is the detailed examination and assessment of an idea or passage.

• Criticize Karl Marx's theory of surplus value.
• Critically analyze Marx's theory of surplus value.

Discuss: Examine an issue from all perspectives and present an argument with supporting evidence.

• Discuss the role of missionaries in southern Africa in the nineteenth century.

Evaluate: Similar in requirements to Assess and Criticize. You may also be required to establish criteria for your evaluation.

• Evaluate Durkheim's theory of deviance.

Explain: Examine and clarify an issue or idea.
• Explain Gandhi's philosophy of Satyagraha.

Some explanatory questions may require developing and substantiating a point of view.

• Explain the failure of Alexander Kerensky's Provisional Government in 1917.

Interpret: Explain the meaning of a passage or quotation. The question usually also requires your assessment of the passage or quotation.

• Interpret the following statement: Freedom is the prerequisite of great art.

Justify: Support an argument or position with evidence and reasons.

• Justify U.S. intervention in Grenada in 1980.

Refute: Oppose an argument or position with evidence and reasons.

• Refute Brenton's contention that "there is a direct correlation between low taxes and violent crime in society."

Trace: Describe developments in narrative or logical order.
• Trace the decline of the League of Nations.

NOTES

1. Lucile V. Payne, *The Lively Art of Writing* (Chicago: Follett, 1965), 19.

2. Harry F. Wolcott, *Writing up Qualitative Research*, Qualitative Research Methods Series, vol. 20 (Newbury Park, CA: Sage Publications, 1990), 69.

3. Alden Todd, *Finding Facts Fast* (Berkeley: Ten Speed Press, 1979), 10.

4. Edward de Bono, *CORT I: Teachers' Notes* (New York: Pergamon, 1973), 7.

5. John M. Good, *The Shaping of Western Society* (New York: Holt, Rinehart, and Winston, 1968), 19.

6. R.J. Shafer, ed., *A Guide to Historical Method* (Homewood, IL: Dorsey Press, 1974), 101.

7. Sheridan Baker, *The Practical Stylist*, 7th ed. (New York: Harper and Row, 1990), 43.

8. William Zinsser, *On Writing Well*, 6th ed. (New York: HarperCollins, 1998), 84.

9. William Strunk and E.B. White, *The Elements of Style*, 4th ed. (Boston: Allyn and Bacon, 2000), 72.

10. Sylvan Barnet and Reid Gilbert, *A Short Guide to Writing about Literature* (New York: Addison-Wesley, 1997), 300.

11. Gordon Taylor, *The Student's Writing Guide for the Arts and Social Sciences* (Melbourne: Cambridge University Press, 1989), 160.

12. Rosalie Maggio, *The Non-Sexist Word Finder: A Dictionary of Gender-Free Usage* (Boston: Beacon, 1988),170.

13. Joseph Gibaldi, ed., *MLA Handbook for Writers of Research Papers,* 5th ed. (New York: MLA, 1999), 33.

14. Payne, 61.

15. Zinsser, 17.

WORKS CONSULTED

American Psychological Association. *Publication Manual.* 4th ed. Washington, D.C: American Psychological Association, 1994.

Barzun, Jacques and Henry F. Graff. *The Modern Researcher.* 5th ed. Boston: Houghton Mifflin, 1992.

The Chicago Manual of Style. 14th ed. Chicago: University of Chicago Press, 1993.

Crouse, Maurice. *Citing Electronic Information in History Papers.* 17 February 2001. <http://www.people. memphis.edu/~mcrouse/elcite.html> (6 March 2001).

Gibaldi, Joseph, ed. *MLA Handbook for Writers of Research Papers.* 5th ed. New York: MLA, 1999.

Harnack, Andrew and Eugene Kleppinger. *Online! A Reference Guide to Using Internet Sources.* New York: St Martin's, 2000.

Maggio, Rosalie. *The Non-Sexist Word Finder: A Dictionary of Gender-Free Usage.* Boston: Beacon, 1988.

Mann, Thomas. *The Oxford Guide to Library Research.* New York: Oxford University Press, 1998.

Sternberg, Robert J. *The Psychologist's Companion.* 3rd ed. New York: Cambridge University Press, 1993.

Strunk, William and E.B. White. *The Elements of Style.* 4th ed. Boston: Allyn and Bacon, 2000.

Taylor, Gordon. *The Student's Writing Guide for the Arts and Social Sciences.* Melbourne: Cambridge University Press, 1989.

Turabian, Kate L. *A Manual for Writers of Term Papers, Theses, and Dissertations.* 6th ed. Chicago: University of Chicago Press, 1996.

_____. *Student's Guide for Writing College Papers.* 3rd ed. Chicago: University of Chicago Press, 1976.

Zinsser, William. *On Writing Well.* 6th ed. New York: HarperCollins, 1998.

INDEX